GHOSTS OF
MOUNT HOLLY

GHOSTS OF MOUNT HOLLY

A HISTORY OF HAUNTED HAPPENINGS

JAN LYNN BASTIEN

Published by Haunted America
A Division of The History Press
Charleston, SC 29403
www.historypress.net

Cover design by Marshall Hudson.
All images by the author unless otherwise noted.

First published 2008

Manufactured in the United Kingdom

ISBN 978.1.59629.372.4

Library of Congress CIP data applied for.

Notice: The information in this book is true and complete to the best of our knowledge. It is offered without guarantee on the part of the author or The History Press. The author and The History Press disclaim all liability in connection with the use of this book.

A portion of the author's royalties from this book will be donated to the Burlington County Animal Alliance, an animal rescue organization in the Mount Holly area, to help provide food, shelter and medical care to abandoned animals in their foster care. This group of dedicated volunteers has worked for almost two decades now to save the lives of thousands of homeless pets, finding them their forever homes and the love and care that every being deserves.

*To my little ones on the other side; may you forever haunt me.
I'll see you at the Rainbow Bridge*

Contents

CONTENTS

Foreword

Sprightly spirits dancing down the lane in the growing evening shade. A wisp of light—or dark—passes just out of view. A vision or a dream telling a story of the remote past. Tales of long ago and not so far away test your rational mind and send a shiver through you. Such things make up a good haunting. Good fun for all—but are they true?

I've never been one to take stock in ghosties and goblins, though I do admit to being regularly scared as a child. Usually this was the result of some movie or story in which my parents had allowed me to indulge my imagination. Still, until I started hosting ghost walks in Mount Holly, I never felt the need to know more.

In *Ghosts of Mount Holly: A History of Haunted Happenings*, Jan Bastien explores the real and the unreal, the good and the ghastly of Mount Holly's past. As she says, some spirits just don't want to leave a pleasant home. Others seem tormented and tied to the locale despite a desire to be elsewhere. Why do some leave only orbs and others appear as lifelike as you and I? Why do we care?

The spirit world has been a part of human existence since we became human. It is the uniquely human tendency to place stock and purpose in our demise; to assure ourselves of a life after we pass from this earth. The spirit world (good and bad) assures us that we have a soul that transcends our actions during our lifetimes and stands long after we fall. It makes for darned good tales as well.

Jan takes these tales of Mount Holly past and brings the spirits into our living rooms. The ghost of the Hessian soldier, long a tradition in the town, takes on new purpose as we look at his demise from his own perspective. The young girl in the library (formerly the Langstaff Mansion) who visits with children during story time on Tuesdays and then disappears when she is discovered. The restive firefighters who respond to a call at the Relief Company, even though there's no fire alarm—in this dimension.

Darn good stories. Or are they? You and I will read on and see just who these spirits are and why they've decided to hang around town for a while. Jan gives you the lead. The reader will need to explore his or her own beliefs and experiences.

Take the lead and walk down the lane. You never know who you might meet.

Dennis C. Rizzo

Preface

"My thinking is that we should all be interested in the paranormal since we'll all be on the other side some day."
–Garden State Ghost Hunters Society website

When you think of haunted cities, towns like Savannah, New Orleans or London come to mind. So, shortly after moving to Mount Holly and seeing a network news truck on High Street, I never thought it would be covering a ghost story in my new hometown. Watching the eleven o'clock news, I was amazed as the reporter announced that ghosts were seen at the old Burlington County Prison Museum. Soon I found myself researching paranormal activity throughout Mount Holly and arranging popular ghost tours here.

"Mount Holly" sounds like such a pleasant place. Its name conjures up serene thoughts of mountains of trees with waxy green leaves and bright red berries. Yet the eerie, desolate moaning of abandoned prisoners in an empty jail; the sighing of lonely, young women dining solitaire in restaurants; fallen firefighters and their dogs calling out to their comrades; the marching of soldiers trapped here since the early battles that won our great nation; and the laughter of children called to an untimely death surround us as we go about our daily business here. The "Mount" itself can be an eerie place, and the "Holly" may be remnants left by a ghost of some Christmas long past.

In Henry Shinn's 1957 *The History of Mount Holly*, Shinn spoke of the few living descendants walking Mount Holly's streets who will "one by one join the company of those that rest in the quiet Friends burying ground, on the sunny slope of the Mount or await judgment day in the serene and peaceful beauty of Iron Works Hill." But many of today's residents and shopkeepers do not believe all of these spirits slumber peacefully beneath headstones. What they've experienced is backed by the findings of investigations led by certified, professional ghost researchers who use the latest equipment and prove that many former Mount Holly inhabitants are not so peaceful and their activities cannot be called "slumbering." It is evident these spirits either cannot or choose not to leave, and many are crying out for recognition.

A quaint county seat, rich in American history, landscaped with award-winning gardens that adorn striking colonial- and Victorian-period architecture, a destination for shopping, dining and year-round events; such is the public face of historic Mount Holly. But do you dare find out about the other side of Mount Holly? Do you dare to walk around the streets of a town that ghost researchers have labeled a "hotbed of ghostly activity"? These are the stories of the people of Mount Holly, the people of today mingling with those who have walked these streets and lived in our homes before us. A town full of history and a sense of community; a place you hate to leave—even when your lease on life has expired.

My undying appreciation goes to those who have helped me create this account of things that go bump in the night, and daylight, in Mount Holly. Many thanks to my friends and neighbors who have taken the time to share their experiences with me. Many of you are mentioned by name on these pages, and if you have remained anonymous, you know that I am thanking you, too. I owe a debt of gratitude, at least six feet deep, to Dennis Rizzo, who referred me to The History Press and who I shamelessly pestered throughout this process, for his advice, preparing images and for sharing his deep knowledge of Mount Holly's history. Thanks to Mike Eck at the Mount Holly Library who helped tremendously with research, and understood when all my books were constantly overdue. Most of all, thanks to my husband, Chas Bastien, who supported me when I put much of my other life on hold while I wrote this book, and fortified me with delicious dinners at night and waffles on Sunday mornings. And a big snuggly head butt to Noah, who always knew when I needed a purr.

Especially, thanks to the ghosts of Mount Holly, who gave life to this book, and to Dave Juliano and Jamie Faith Eachus at South Jersey Ghost Research, and Tim and Marisa Bozarth at Garden State Ghost Hunters Society, who have dedicated much of their lives to finding these lingering spirits and have generously shared their knowledge with me.

What Are You Afraid Of?

"Ya Gotta Believe!"
—Tug McGraw, relief pitcher for the Philadelphia Phillies and New York Mets

Many recent surveys claim that there are more Americans believing in ghosts, or some form of the paranormal, than not. Paranormal beliefs have been studied from many angles, from age and education to religious and political persuasion (yes, the Harris poll surveyed Democrats versus Republicans). The results almost always find the majority believing that ghosts and other paranormal anomalies do exist, regardless of other beliefs or demographics. Long gone are the days when old-fashioned superstitions and tea leaf readings were considered scientific, yet poll results today show the trend toward believing in the spook-tacular is not diminishing with modern advances in science or technology. A 2001 report by Hughes, Behanna and Signorella in the *Journal of Social Psychology* claims paranormal beliefs have remained stable or increased since the 1970s. Results of 2001 and 2005 Gallup surveys compiled by David Moore claim that at least 76 percent of Americans believe in some form of the paranormal. Interestingly, a poll similar to the Gallup poll and conducted by Britt at Oklahoma City University produced results showing that the more educated you are, the more your tendency to believe in the paranormal may increase.

The 2005 Gallup survey compiled by Moore shows the most popular paranormal beliefs lean toward extrasensory perception (ESP) at 41 percent and haunted houses, which claim the believers at 37 percent of the population. Right behind that is believing that spirits of dead people can come back in certain places or situations, belief in telepathy, clairvoyance and astrology. Belief in witches, reincarnation and that people can communicate mentally with someone who has died also garnered at least 20 percent of the American population's credence.

Every Friday the thirteenth, Main Street Mount Holly hosts the Haunted Holly Ghost Tour, a ghost walk visiting at least seven public buildings that have been certified to be haunted by South Jersey Ghost Research (SJGR). No private homes are on the tour, yet many Mount Holly homeowners claim to be cohabitating with a spirit or two. As part of the tour, a presentation on ghost hunting and communicating with those who have crossed over is provided. The popularity of this ghost tour, the many ghost tours in cities across the United States and Europe, the increase in paranormal television shows, websites, books and other media presentations all seem to indicate that the general public, if not necessarily believing in ghosts, certainly has a strong interest in the possibility that they do exist.

Believing in the different forms of the supernatural is prevalent throughout the history of mankind. The reason given most frequently for believing in ghosts is having had a personal paranormal or telepathic experience, according to Paola Bressman. Fear of death often pervades life itself, fueling the interest in what could happen after death. Ghost stories have been told in almost all cultures since ancient times and have been handed down through the centuries in various forms, from writing on the walls of caves and medieval literature to today's campfire tales and urban myths. Today, paranormal research groups employing a wide range of state-of-the-art equipment and scientific approaches to investigation are able to determine whether the things that go bump in the night could actually be caused by spirit activity or are just figments of an overstressed imagination. Reports of their findings are accessible to many via the Internet and on many modern television programs about ghost hunting. Indeed, the number of websites posted by paranormal research groups and TV programs featuring the paranormal is growing as fast as the waiting list for sold-out Haunted Holly Ghost Tour tickets!

Being able to have a paranormal experience is sometimes dependant on how sensitive you are. "Sensitive" is a word SJGR Director Dave Juliano likes to use in place of "psychic," and it refers to your openness to receiving messages from the spirit world. Being sensitive allows you to rely on your gut feelings and recognize the signs the spirits send you. Everyone has these abilities, and maybe it will happen to you just once in your lifetime, or maybe it will happen many times. Sometimes it depends on having the right conditions for it to happen, staying calm and being open to the possibility. "Everyone has the potential to see or sense a spirit," writes Juliano in *Ghost Research 101*.

If you are brave enough to consider having a personal paranormal experience, and participate in a ghost tour in Mount Holly or another spooky town, what are the types of paranormal energy you might encounter? Let's meet some of these characters and see what makes them haunt. Many of these have been found here in Mount Holly.

Residual energy is energy that has been imprinted on an area or building that recurs when the conditions are right. Dave Juliano likens it to playing a video over and over. While you may see the event being played in front of you, there is no interaction between you and the spirit(s); they do not even know you are there. While it may be frightening, you are in no danger. "Gettysburg is a good example of this. You see the soldiers marching; it doesn't change," says Jamie Faith Eachus, SJGR's assistant director. Juliano explains that earth and stone are good conduits for this residual energy.

An *interactive spirit* often manifests as an apparition or partial apparition. This is the spirit of a deceased human being (or sometimes an animal). This type of spirit occurs more frequently than an apparition, and can be marked by footsteps or other sounds, odors, orbs or mists. Those whom are visited by an interactive spirit also claim to have been physically touched by an unseen hand or to have felt a temperature fluctuation.

An *earthbound spirit* is the spirit of someone who has not yet crossed over; it is "stuck." There are many reasons for this. The spirit may not realize he is dead, or he may need to complete unfinished business before he is ready to cross over. Maybe he is afraid to cross over, afraid of hell, judgment or just the unknown. Sometimes a spirit can't cross because it feels guilty for leaving a loved one behind; in fact, a living person can also contribute to this guilt and stop a loved one from crossing over. Sometimes a sudden death may have confused a spirit and it can't accept that it has died. It remains to try to catch the attention of sensitives in the area. This type of spirit can be found almost anywhere a death has occurred, according to Juliano.

Whether these earthbound spirits or interactive spirits are good or bad, helpful or harmful, often depends on the type of person they were when they were alive.

Demons represent various kinds of spirits, both good and evil, that can intervene in your affairs. In Christianity, it is believed they are the employees of Satan, tormenting people and tempting them to sin, while other religions attribute them with good, bad or dual natures, writes Rosemary Guiley in *The Encyclopedia of Ghosts and Spirits*.

Then we have *poltergeists*, a term that comes from the German words *poltern* ("to knock") and *geist* ("spirit"). This is a mischievous and often malevolent spirit energy, sometimes characterized by creating noises and throwing objects. Poltergeist activity usually starts and stops suddenly and is often centered on or directed at one person, called the "agent." The assaults can be as bad as rock and dirt throwing, physical and sexual assaults, light bulbs spinning in their sockets, telephones repeatedly dialing the same number and offensive smells. Some cases have been linked with demonic possession and typically have been cured by exorcism, Guiley explains. Fortunately, there have been no reports of poltergeists on the Haunted Holly Ghost Tour, and Dave Juliano feels that true poltergeist hauntings are very rare and that a person could be "causing the entire poltergeist problem with their subconscious mind and they are not aware they are the cause."

Are you one of the three out of every four who believes in ghosts? Come visit Mount Holly's ghosts and let them convince you. Decide if it is residual energy or interactive spirits talking to you. What's the matter—are you scared?

A "Skeleton" of
Mount Holly History

"For who can wonder that man should feel a vague belief in tales of disembodied spirits wandering through those places which they once dearly affected, when he himself, scarcely less separated from his old world than they, is for ever lingering upon past emotions and bygone times, and hovering, the ghost of his former self, about the places and people that warmed his heart of old?"
—*Charles Dickens,* Master Humphrey's Clock

As you walk down High Street, Garden Street or any street in Mount Holly, you are standing on a battleground of the American Revolution, walking over the sites where American, British or Hessian soldiers have fallen, crossing by the paths of the Underground Railroad and strolling past the cells of executed criminals. You may be near the playground of long-gone children, an overgrown village of Lenni Lenape Indians, the gardens of Victorian socialites or the factories of long-ago ironworks that forged "iron pots and implements" for the colonial soldiers of the Revolution, as Dennis Rizzo describes in *Mount Holly, New Jersey: A Hometown Reinvented.* Today's quaint shops and galleries once were the homes of farmers and factory workers, the library was once the mansion of a wealthy landowner and an eerie museum was once the longest continuously operating prison of convicted felons. While, according to author Rizzo, the town has been "reinvented," the past also remains. And so may its past inhabitants.

Mount Holly was a theater of the American Revolution, with the Redcoats twice taking over the Friends Meeting House, the Thomas Budd House and many other buildings and residences in town. The Battle of Iron Works Hill in Mount Holly was a diversionary tactic to keep Colonel Von Donop preoccupied here in December of 1776, while Washington's haggard, hungry and ill-equipped troops went on to fight the Battle of Trenton. This plan succeeded because, writes Rizzo, while Von Donop was celebrating his success in Mount Holly, Washington claimed victory at Trenton. Von Donop was an eight-hour march away when courier brought him the news, and there was little he could do at that juncture to alter this segment of history, often called the turning point of the American Revolution. While the frustrated British and Hessians burned and ransacked Mount Holly buildings in retaliation, including the ironworks at Saint Andrew's Cemetery, many of these colonial structures still remain today, surviving the orders of General Henry Clinton in 1778 to destroy and plunder. What also remains are apparitions of Hessian and colonial soldiers, the sound of marching boots and even the emotions and body odor of weary warriors; all have been seen and sensed in several Mount Holly buildings.

While history is reenacted on the streets of Mount Holly, some of the real players have never left.

But before the Europeans ever set foot in Mount Holly, before they had a colony to fight for, this land and this town belonged to the Lenni Lenape Indians, who settled along the Rancocas Creek (they called it the Ankokus) in longhouses and huts, sometimes pulling up stakes to take advantage of seasonal food. First to their land came the Dutch and the Swedes, who settled around the area looking to expand their trapping trade. Relatively few in numbers, they didn't bother the Indians much. But when a boatload of English settlers arriving in Burlington aboard the *Kent* initiated the influx of colonial settlers to the area in the 1670s, it was the beginning of the end of life as they knew it for the Lenni Lenapes. Along with their different culture, religious beliefs and desires for land acquisition, these pale-faced settlers also brought foreign diseases to the land of the Lenape. By the mid-1700s, the indigenous tribes of the Mount Holly area had vaporized to a memory. Today, a reservation of the Powhatan Renape Nation, which sits at the edge of Mount Holly, is about all that remains of Native American tradition in this area, Rizzo writes.

With easy transportation to Philadelphia via the Rancocas Creek and the Delaware River, Mount Holly's commerce grew. With fertile grounds, so did farms and plantations. The mill raceways were dug to provide power and the creek was used to transport goods to Philadelphia from the mills and furnaces that sprung up during the commercial and industrial growth of the area, while shops and markets flourished on the streets. In his book *The Jersey Midlands*, Henry Beck relates that steamer ships toured the Rancocas on daily schedules and women often boarded for a daytrip to Philadelphia, taking their knitting and sewing with them.

This boom town of the eighteenth century was not always called Mount Holly, as Elizabeth Perinchief explains in *History of Cemeteries in Burlington County*:

> *This was originally called Northampton Township and Mt Holly was one of the early towns in the township. This original township covered one half of the area of the county from Burlington Township to the borders of Atlantic and Ocean Counties. At the present time because of the many townships that were taken from it, it is one of the smallest. The town of Mt. Holly, from which the present township takes its name covers the entire area—2.9 square miles. The original township dated back to 1688.*
>
> *The town of Mt. Holly was also known as Bridgetown in the early days. Because of its location at the head of the north branch of the Rancocas Creek, there was good water power and the then navigable creek made transportation of products to and from the Delaware comparatively cheap and easy.*

The town's lovely name was bestowed upon it by John Cripps, one of the first area landowners and a passenger aboard the *Kent*. When settlers surveyed land back then, they noted landmarks by what existed, and since there were not many streets and buildings at the time, natural landmarks were often used, like "Cripps's Oak," a large, white oak tree that stood until recently at the intersection of Garden and Branch Streets, in which Cripps carved his initials. Another surveyor's mark at the northern end of town is a hill that became known as "The Mount." Cripps was impressed with its beauty rising above the plains, crowned with holly trees, writes Shinn in *The History of Mount Holly*. Hence, Cripps designated the area "Mount Holly."

The town grew, churches were established and fire departments and state and local government departments were organized, as well as social and business organizations. Restaurants, hotels, taverns and shopping districts grew in numbers with the residences. The railroad came to town, augmenting the steamboat trade here and increasing opportunities for economic prosperity. The county fair drew crowds from its inception in the mid-1800s and for many decades to come.

Mount Holly was home to a large Quaker population that first met in homes or traveled to Burlington to worship, and then built its own meetinghouse here at Garden and High Street. While slavery was allowed in New Jersey through the eighteenth century, the Friends were uncomfortable with the practice, and leaders in their congregation, notably John Woolman, whose memorial still stands in Mount Holly today, led the charge for its abolition in the region. His efforts and writings were a driving force behind the Act for the Gradual Abolition of Slavery in New Jersey, in 1804, according to Rizzo.

Mount Holly was a stop on the Underground Railroad. Slaves fleeing to refuge in New York and Canada passed through Mount Holly from Maryland's Eastern Shore, and they often found refuge in a Mount Holly community known as Timbuctoo, Rizzo writes. A small cemetery and a few houses remain where this hamlet stood, and stories of ghosts there have been handed down for the past century or so.

While the War Between the States was not fought on Mount Holly soil, many former Mount Holly residents volunteered to serve in this sorrowful Civil War and residents here continue to this day to defend our country in the skirmishes our nation finds itself in. The proximity of Fort Dix and McGuire Air Force Base have made the presence of the military very familiar to Mount Holly, with many members of our armed forces calling Mount Holly their home, at least temporarily. Still, the Quaker influence here continues to make its feelings known, with banners preaching sentiments such as "There is no way to peace; peace is the way" flying alongside the

Friends Meeting House, one of our haunted buildings. Yet many Mount Holly ghost reports are of soldiers, and one can only speculate which battles these poor souls endured, or possibly lost their lives to.

Mount Holly, one of the oldest towns in the United States, has endured the ups and downs of the American economy, prospered during the Industrial Revolution and suffered during the Depression and the more recent flight to the suburbs and shopping malls. Today, through the efforts of its citizens who recognize the value of a small-town neighborhood, the new merchants pumping vitality into the economy alongside those who have stood by through the hard times, the artists who have discovered the gem in the rough they continue to polish until it shines, Mount Holly is a destination for artists, antique hunters, shoppers and diners, and home again to those seeking a sense of community.

Through all this history and through all these changes in culture, lifestyle and tradition, many lives have left something behind, many emotions have been exposed or repressed, many longings and memories still remain. Many are clinging to a spirit they will not allow to cross; over, many will not cross until they complete something they left undone.

A town so rich in history is bound to be wealthy in ghosts as well. "Haunted locations are haunted because the energy required for the haunting activity is available due to long time human occupancy under the expense of extreme emotions," states Tom Butler in his dissertation to the 2007 conference of the Academy of Spirituality and Paranormal Studies. Wars, tragedy, slavery and imprisonment are all emotional environments that hinder peaceful rest. Then maybe the prosperous good times keep some spirits here because they enjoyed life so much, or maybe some hang around for the changes because they don't want to miss anything.

"Mount Holly is a hotbed of spirit activity," claims Dave Juliano, director of South Jersey Ghost Research. Whatever the reason, history here just doesn't seem to leave!

The Old Burlington County Prison

"The inmates are ghosts whose dreams have been murdered…"
—Jill Johnston, journalist, observing patients in a mental ward
at New York's Bellevue Hospital

I wonder why they stay in prison. I'd want to return to a happier place in my life." This thought of the ghosts lingering at her work site has haunted Burlington County Prison Museum's curator, Marisa Bozarth. The Prison Museum is located on High Street, in the center of historic Mount Holly. "When I see a shadow walking by, I want to know what they are doing. Do they see me?"

Now open only as a museum and listed as a National Historic Landmark, the imposing gray stone walls of the Burlington County Prison stand adjacent to the original courthouse of Burlington County. The prison lists among its alumni such dignitaries as Albert DeSalvo, aka the "Boston Strangler," who did a two-day stint here on a rape charge in January of 1955.

Designed by one of America's first native-born and trained architects, Robert Mills, also designer of the Washington Monument, the Burlington County Prison was completed in 1811. With the interior vaulted ceilings of poured concrete and its brick and stone construction, the building was virtually fireproof, and looked as dismal as the hopes and souls of those who inhabited it. The outside of the building has changed very little. The word PRISON in huge letters carved in stone above the massive front door laden with heavy hinges and large lock is as it was the day the prison first opened. The interior is whitewashed, as it would have been when first occupied. The cell doors are also original and many were fabricated in place. The prison is so well constructed that it remained in constant use until 1965, making it the longest continually operated prison in the United States, boasts the Burlington County Prison Museum's brochure. A home to many lost souls of this life and beyond, the words and deeds of its many guests remain alive in the graffiti preserved on some of the walls, and with the frequent paranormal activity within its stone cells and passageways and in the courtyard behind the building.

The "dungeon," or maximum-security cell, was in the center of the top floor. That location was carefully chosen to prevent escape by digging, to minimize communication with criminals in the cell blocks and to ensure constant surveillance by guards making rounds. This was the only cell without a fireplace. It is flanked by niches for guards or visitors and has one very high, very small window and an iron ring in the center of the floor to which the prisoner could be chained. It was also known as cell #5.

Despite its heavy security (at least for those times), a few escapes were attempted, and some were successful. One partially successful escape occurred in 1875, when five men attempted a breakout. In the far corner of the third-floor bathroom, they cut a hole in the ceiling and kicked in the roof. The first four made it out, but as they were trying to pull the last inmate through, the commotion got the attention of the guards. The first two ran away and were never found. The other two that got out, and the one stuck in the roof, were captured and returned to their cells. In 1954,

Today a museum, the Burlington County Prison Museum once housed the tortured souls of inmates.

three men being held in one cell on the top floor for liquor theft charges escaped by sawing through the bars with piano wire and soap. It is believed the piano wire was snuck in to them by a visitor. They were never caught, according to an interview with Marisa Bozarth.

Eight men and one woman were executed while serving time in the prison. Also, in 1920, a guard was murdered there by an inmate. Let's listen to the tales of some of these lost lives; could their tortured souls still be imprisoned in the cells that arrested their spirits? Many believe so, and some experts have proof.

On July 6, 1833, Joel Clough came to this prison a broken man, a perpetrator of a crime of passion. Hopelessly in love with Mary Hamilton of Bordentown, the widowed daughter of his landlord, he repeatedly proposed marriage to her and threatened to commit suicide if she would not marry him. One night, after being jilted again, his passion overcame him and in a fit of anger and frustration, he stabbed her to death. In his confession, Clough admitted, "On the day of the fatal deed, I had retired to my chamber with gloomy and desperate thoughts. My mind contemplated both her destruction and my own." When Mrs. Hamilton checked on Clough in his room because she thought he was ill, he pulled a dagger from his pocket, which he admits he "had taken from the drawer for the double purpose of murder and suicide." He stabbed her repeatedly, yet never killed himself. According to the Association of the Bar of the City of New York, the defense counsel vainly argued that Clough was temporarily insane, and Clough stated he had not meant to kill the object of his love, but his passion was so intense that it got the better of him. He admitted in his confession, which is on file at the Burlington County Prison Museum, that he was "impartially tried and justly sentenced; and am now to suffer the merited punishment of my crime."

While awaiting his execution, Clough found religion and was visited by pastors of several faiths. He was initially assigned to the dungeon, but he protested and declared he could not enter the cell alive. Prison officials must have eventually taken pity on him and allowed him candles and moved him to a more comfortable cell, also on the second floor, so that he could receive his visitors of the cloth. In appreciation for their compassion, Clough broke out of prison on the morning of Sunday, July 21, 1833, only to be captured in Burlington along the river later that night as he tried to make his way to Philadelphia. He was then returned to the prison, where he was chained in the dungeon with double irons and a guard watch set over him. Of his escape, Clough remarked to prison officials, "You know, gentlemen, that life is sweet, and who there is that would not do anything that would not afford him the least chance of saving it, but now, gentlemen, I am done—and shall endeavor to give it up...now all is over and I hope to be able to prepare myself for another world."

Clough "gave it up" on July 26, 1833, at 2:30 p.m., before an audience of about 1,200 people. He was executed by hanging at a site about two miles from the Burlington County Prison, on a road then known as Philadelphia Road (today it is Route 537, locally known as Marne Highway), between Mount Holly and Hainesport. Climbing the platform and assisting the sheriff as he placed the noose around his neck, at twenty-nine years of age, Joel Clough left this world behind. After his body hung for about thirty minutes, it was cut down, placed in a mahogany coffin and taken to the prison grounds, where he was buried behind the courtyard. Immediately upon Clough's death, inmates started complaining of moaning and other sounds coming from Clough's former cell. This was the beginning of reported hauntings at the prison, tales which continue today.

Over half a century later, another crime of passion resulted in a sentence to the prison. In the early morning hours of September 18, 1892, Wesley Warner lay in wait for his lover, Lizzie Peak, who he believed to be unfaithful, to return from the opera house with her sisters. His suspicions, to him, were confirmed, as she came walking down Pine Street with her two sisters and three male escorts, whom they had picked up on their way back from the show. Prior to his stakeout, Warner had spent some time at the bar at Vanscivers Hotel (currently the Mill Street Tavern) and also at Lizzie's parents' home. He had in his possession a bottle of fiery rum from Vanscivers and a butcher knife he had found hidden under a stack of dirty dishes at the Peak residence.

His jealousy raged as the merrymakers approached, and as his suspicions of her unfaithfulness actualized before his eyes, Warner jumped out of the bushes, screamed, "Oh, God damn you!" and lunged at Lizzie with the knife. One of her sisters' escorts, Thomas Shinn, went after Warner with a fence paling, but Warner got away from them. Lizzie was taken to the home of Joseph F. Bryan, where she was found to be dead and then taken to undertaker Keeler in the morning, according to the Burlington County Prison Museum's reprint of "A History of Wesley Warner's Crime."

Warner spent the night at a friend's home on Water Street (now Rancocas Road), left about 5:00 a.m. and tried to hire a livery service to Philadelphia. Since he had no money for the fare, he was not able to skip town and was arrested later that morning by Officer Robert M. Brown, who transported him to jail.

A grand jury found Wesley Warner guilty. His trial was held in December and at every session, the old Burlington County Court House, still in use today and located next to the prison, was filled to capacity. On January 9, 1893, Warner was sentenced to be hanged the following March. However, several appeals delayed his execution, and his stay at the prison was extended. While there, Warner refused to believe he would suffer the death penalty. He acted haughtily, ate heartily and slept soundly. Meals were provided to him by Landlord Zelley of the Washington House. Warner refused all religious consolation and insisted on his right to another trial. He was under constant surveillance.

On Thursday morning, September 6, 1894, Reverend J. Madison Hare of Burlington was sent to Warner's cell by officials for a final religious consolation. The previous day, Warner had received visits from his barber and three brothers; his mother did not feel she could make the trip. His conversations that last full day of his life had been filled with expletives and rambling conversation. Finally, on this morning of his execution, Warner lost his composure and collapsed. Recovering, he dressed for the occasion and then walked solemnly with Sheriff Townsend to his execution, which was to be held at a scaffold constructed in the northeast corner of the courtyard of the prison, behind a stone wall. It was an area where prisoners held for minor offenses often took their exercise. A large crowd of both men and women gathered outside the jail. As the straps were placed around his legs and the black cap was adjusted on his head, Wesley Warner uttered his final words: "Gentlemen, you will all be sorry for this. I thank Mr. Hare for what he has done for me. Good bye, Mr. Hare, good bye all. Here goes to the only begotten son."

The book on Warner's crime also reports of other executions at the Burlington County Prison. One was Philip Lynch, who was executed here in 1859 for murdering a drinking buddy, George Coulter, in Bordentown. Their last binge together resulted in a fight on the way home from the bar and Lynch left Coulter in a heap on the side of the road. Then he returned home, got a gun, went back and finished Coulter by beating him to death with the stock of the rifle. He later denied any knowledge of the crime. He was arrested and tried. Upon his conviction, he swore at Judge Van Dyke with burning eyes, threatening vengeance upon the judge, saying, "May the devil die with ye!" Lynch was hanged on March 23, 1860, at a gallows erected on the southeast corner of the jail yard, before a large crowd of spectators, including the National Guard of Mount Holly and the Marion Rifles of Burlington.

In November of 1920, prison guard William Harry King went downstairs to medicate a prisoner who was feigning illness. He entered the basement and there, across from the workshop, he was met by his patient, Harry Asay. Asay waited for Officer King with an iron fireplace poker in his hand, and killed King with his first blow to the head. Asay was sentenced to death for his crime and is buried on the prison grounds. Also killed in the melee was inmate Vernon Bartlett, who was serving time for being drunk and disorderly. Bartlett was working in the kitchen at the time and Asay dealt him a blow with the poker as well. He died later that day of internal injuries in the hospital, according to Marisa Bozarth. King was survived by his wife and two children, whom he had lived with in Burlington, and was buried in his family's plot in Burlington. In 2005 he was named to the National Wall for Fallen Officers in Washington, D.C. Locally, he is honored on a monument for fallen police officers and firemen, located in neighboring Westampton, behind the Fire Training Academy.

In 1965, the heavy doors of the Burlington County prison closed. Its 154 years of housing tormented, condemned souls were over and its intimidating, gray stone walls stood cold and silent. Or did they? Many speculate that though it closed its doors, it is still the home to many spirits left over from the confinement, murders and hangings of days past. Ask Marisa Bozarth, who has been the curator of this prison-turned-museum since July of 2003. She has seen a man run down the hall and someone else run up the stairs. She's heard pacing high heels in the main hallway. But dead men and women have been doing more than just walking around the prison, and reports of their presences lingering here started with the execution of Joel Clough in 1833 and continued until the prison's closing in 1965. Guards often reported hearing chains rattling, smelling cigarette smoke when nobody was smoking and even seeing cigarettes floating around without any visible person holding them.

In 1999, Burlington County decided to renovate the prison and reopen it as a museum. Workers were assigned to make renovations. These men were plagued by a "prankster" who kept hiding their tools. When they discovered the missing tools behind doors that hadn't been opened in years, ghost stories sprang to life and the work slowed down considerably. So the county freeholders summoned South Jersey Ghost Research (SJGR) to the scene, expecting to exorcize the fears of the workers. But their hopes were vaporized when SJGR arrived with their ghost-detecting paraphernalia and confirmed that spirit energies do remain in the prison, forty years after its closing. In fact, the sight has become a favorite haunt of SJGR; they've visited at least ten times, and the historic building is the focal point of interest for several other ghost research groups as well. Paranormal activity is so rampant here in this deserted prison that many paranormal research groups use it as a training grounds for new recruits, because each trip almost always yields "activity," reports Bozarth.

About a dozen different professional ghost research groups have investigated the prison, some from as far away as New York State and Ohio. Apparitions have been spotted on several occasions, as well as temperature fluctuations and electronic spikes detected on equipment. Orbs dot photos and voices on tapes call out, "I'm over here" or, "I'm on the stairs."

Graffiti of former prisoners are like messages from the grave. *Photo by Larry Tigar.*

Bozarth explains, "The voices are decibels below what you can hear…but they show up on tape. You can also tell that the voices are below what a human could produce. They're usually mumbled, but you can hear they're trying to tell you where they are."

Who could actually be haunting the prison is anyone's guess, but Joel Clough is always theorized as the most likely candidate and others are suspected. It was where Clough spent his last night alive, and his body is buried on the prison grounds. After Clough's death, inmates claimed they heard moaning, the sound of chains rattling and the bars of the dungeon shaking. The ghost research groups always confirm activity around his former cell. Dave Juliano, director of South Jersey Ghost Research, believes Clough's spirit remains here, since "that's when it all started. He is probably stuck, and too scared to cross over." Juliano reports that motion sensors always go off around the dungeon, even though there is nothing in the room that would move, and voice recorders capture moaning in cell #5.

Some believe the ghost of murdered prison guard William Harry King still roams these stone hallways. The ghost busters always confirm activity outside the basement workshop where Officer King was murdered. Many investigators have reported feeling overcome with sadness in this area, some to the point of crying themselves.

Visitors report sightings here as well. One steamy summer day in 2002, Alicia McShulkis decided to take her son, John, and a fifth-grade classmate on a tour through the prison museum. When they got there, they were told the fans and the air conditioning were not working. "All the better," thought Alicia. "The boys can experience what it was like in the summer here in the 1800s." The kids loved roaming the halls of the prison, imagining the inmates who occupied the dreary cells for so many years. Then they went down to the basement. As they approached the cell where King was murdered by Asay, Alicia saw a hand come through the bars of the cell. John's pal saw it, too. Quickly, they fled the premises. Alicia still acts as one of the guides for the Haunted Holly Ghost Tour, but she claims that she will not go back to this area of the prison anymore.

While it is only speculated as to who does actually haunt this eerie building, all paranormal research groups who have investigated the prison are certain the spirits exist. South Jersey Paranormal Research's website has a clip of voices captured in the basement that sounds like various voices calling off the names, "Waters, Mulford, Rutmeuler, Edgars…" The basement is where the kitchen was located, and after the roll call you can hear a woman's voice saying, "I shoulda washed plates."

During an interview in August 2007, Bozarth told of the day when the descendants of Wesley Warner visited the museum in 2003. "I think that his spirit has been in the prison in the past. We had one instance when his relatives came into the jail. The atmosphere in the building changed and they said that they felt like they were being followed. Once they left, the feelings of being followed and watched disappeared."

Bozarth said that one time when South Jersey Paranormal Research investigated the prison, the lights blinked off and on in a way that is impossible to do manually with the wiring in the prison. When someone got scared and asked the ghosts to stop, they did. "No harm is done and nobody's been touched. It's mostly energy stuff," says Bozarth. Also during that investigation, pounding was heard on the front door, but nobody was there.

On an investigation by Garden State Ghost Hunters Society in May 2005, researchers equipped with 35-millimeter cameras with 400 speed film or higher, digital cameras, laser thermometers, two EMF detectors, a hand-held camcorder with night vision, two still cameras, tape recorders and dowsing rods visited the prison. They detected cold spots in the basement where Officer King was murdered. One investigator was overcome with feelings of sorrow there. Outside in the courtyard, a leader of the group pinpointed an indentation in the ground where she felt "the prisoner is buried that killed the guard." She also felt that there is more than one body buried in the courtyard. Dowsing rods used by two investigators to detect magnetic fields began to cross as soon as they walked into the indent, and they also kept pointing in the direction of the indent when they walked near it. It is true that Clough, as well as Harry Asay and possibly others, is buried there. In a night vision video on the second floor near the dungeon, where Clough was housed, the investigators were able to film a video of a "ghost face" coming out of the wall, according to their website.

South Jersey Ghost Research always finds activity when they investigate the prison. They come with state-of-the-art equipment, including cameras, motion detectors, thermometers and voice recorders, which they carefully documented in all their reports, along with other factors of the investigation such as weather conditions of the night. On their many visits, typical findings have included electronic voice phenomena producing sounds like spirits asking questions. "What is it?" one woman's voice said. "Deny it," said another voice. Responding to the investigators' questions of "Is anybody there?" a voice said, "No." SJGR's Juliano said his group also had the heavy feelings of despair when investigating the basement where King was murdered.

Bozarth and her husband Tim are both members of the Garden State Ghost Hunters Society, and Tim is a true skeptic. He says that is why he joined the group. Hearing all the stories from everyone, including his wife, he had to get some solid proof, so he began investigating with the Garden State Ghost Hunters Society, using modern equipment and working with teams experienced in paranormal research.

The fact that he saw an apparition float down the hallway of the prison on New Year's Eve of 2003 made Bozarth start to consider that the stories his wife brought home from work may have some substance. But it was one particular incident that truly convinced him that the prison is loaded with spirit activity: a time he brought a medium to the prison. The group brought the psychic to where they were investigating in the bathroom on the third floor. The psychic began telling them that she was speaking with a man she was seeing, who was apparently stuck in the ceiling. She asked him questions about who he was and why he was there, and he said that he was trying to get out. She asked him where his friends were and he apparently said that they had left him there. But two were trying to help him. The psychic said that his name was John, which is one of the names of the people who had attempted the escape through the roof in this very spot in 1875.

The reason this made Tim believe that ghosts truly haunt the prison is because although there is a sign posted in the prison about the escape, it is posted in another room and does not tell the details. The psychic did not see the sign, and even if she did, the details of the event are not posted anywhere and are not widely known. The sign does not mention the names of any of the inmates involved. Tim and Marisa prompted the psychic with some questions, because they knew the details of the escape. The fact that the psychic saw the ghost, identified him and heard the replies that she did, while knowing nothing previously of the event, began to convince

Not all who roam these eerie hallways are on the same spiritual dimension. *Photo by Larry Tigar.*

skeptical Tim Bozarth that the stories of footsteps his wife tells him about and shadows that follow her around her workplace are, indeed, the calling cards of those lost souls from a century or more ago.

While the professional ghost researchers are skeptical and look for positive signs of paranormal activity, many others are intrigued with the overall scariness of this place and capitalize on its spooky appeal. In October, the Prison Museum Association, in coordination with the county freeholders, hosts a fundraiser at the prison. A theatrical group comes in and transforms the historic landmark into a theater of the macabre. Actors dressed like goblins and monsters, ghoulish props and mechanisms and eerie noises to make people jump in shock are around every corner. A maze in the courtyard beckons you to follow through its twists and turns to meet scary creatures lying in wait for their chance to scare you. All the while, many are completely unaware that they are probably trampling over the graves of Joel Clough and Harry Asay. The event is a great fundraiser to keep the prison museum in operation, as lines of people stretching several blocks wait for their chance to scream. The frightening theatrics may be thrilling, but the fact that you are walking over the former inmates' graves and strolling the very grounds that they did (and still do), the proven findings of the scientific ghost researchers and the ghostly things that happen on normal days at this historic site are all far scarier than any spine-chilling experience makeup and props could ever fabricate.

Mount Holly Library
and Lyceum

"Always read something that will make you look good if you die in the middle of it."
—P.J. O'Rourke, American journalist

In the early to mid-1800s, most of the supplies for the entire town of Mount Holly were transported on water and brought into town via the Rancocas Creek. Rizzo reports that there were many steamboat landings along the creek and one was owned by James Langstaff, a wealthy farmer. From his personal landing, which was on Washington Street, Mr. Langstaff brought in materials to build his beautiful estate on High Street, now number 307 and the address of the Mount Holly Library, officially known as the Burlington County Lyceum of History and Natural Sciences.

Built in 1829, this striking example of Georgian architecture boasts fireplaces made of Pennsylvania blue marble mined at King of Prussia, random-width floorboards of North Carolina yellow pine and iron fireplace firebacks. As you enter the building, you immediately notice the beautiful, open-well winding staircase ahead of you, circling to the third floor. It is topped by a ladder leading to the widow's walk, and then another ladder leading to the captain's walk, as described by the Daughters of the American Revolution in *Historic Mount Holly: The Holly Tour.*

The current Mount Holly Library evolved from two organizations, the Library Company of Bridgetown and the Burlington County Lyceum of History and Natural Sciences, write Rizzo and Shinn in their historical accounts about the library's evolution. In June of 1765, the Library Company of Bridgetown (Mount Holly was called Bridgetown at that time because of its many bridges traversing the Rancocas Creek) received a charter from King George III through William Franklin, son of Ben, and then governor-

The beautiful Mount Holly Library
and Lyceum claimed the life of a little
girl who still visits the children there.

general of New Jersey. At that time, the "library" consisted of a collection
of books that were kept on a shelf at the town hall, then located on Mill
Street. After the town hall was torn down in 1798, the library was moved
from place to place about town. In 1860, a small group of men interested
in local history and the sciences founded the Burlington County Lyceum
of History and Natural Sciences, which included a circulating library, and
came to assume the role of the town library. Interest in preserving the
Lyceum dwindled with the death of many original members, and in 1931
its collection was sent to the state museum in Trenton, to be returned if the
town ever acquired a suitable building. Mount Holly's library is the fifth
oldest in the state, but it wasn't until 1957 that it got its first permanent
home at the former Langstaff mansion. Mike Eck, director of the Mount
Holly Library, says that in addition to a modern collection, the Mount
Holly Library and Lyceum also houses the original Library of Bridgetown
collection of about 155 books, the original charter with the royal signature
and the ghost of a little girl.

She has been reported to come out when children's programs are in
session. Many have seen her peek around the corner at the children seated
in circles reading from their books or listening to stories being told by the
program leader. Does she long to sit down with the children and join in the
games and learning? Who could she be?

A little girl was killed in this building. She fell over the railing through this massive, open winding staircase, plummeting to her death three floors below. She was Cornelia, the eleven-and-a-half-year-old granddaughter of James Langstaff, the original owner of the mansion. She was visiting her grandparents with her family when the accident happened. It is believed that it is Cornelia who appears in the library, peeking around the corner at the other children. She must be longing to take part in the children's programs, maybe beckoning them to play in the yard behind the library that was once her grandparents' estate. She seems to yearn for the company of other children and the play days she missed when her own life was cut short by the tragic fall from her grandparents' staircase over a century ago. The missing piece of railing, reportedly broken during Cornelia's fall, remains missing to this day. If you climb to the third floor, you will see it.

Barb Johns of the Mount Holly library staff, who also sometimes acts as a Haunted Holly Ghost Tour guide, tells about how the front door sometimes creaks and makes a sound like a woman calling; some think this is Annie, Cornelia's stepmother.

South Jersey Ghost Research (SJGR) was summoned to the library to investigate the possibility of paranormal stirrings here in 2005. On January 29, a cold, cloudy evening, six investigators showed up with ghost detecting equipment to conduct the investigation. One investigator felt activity around the staircase, and it was here that his Trifield Natural EM meter detected activity early in the investigation, according to the SJGR website. This type of electromagnetic field meter (EMF) is very sensitive, containing filters that eliminate man-made sources of EMFs, making this type of evidence more significant than using other similar equipment, reports Juliano in *Ghost Research 101*. In this same staircase area, another investigator felt that someone was watching her, and she took photos when she sensed this. Orbs appeared on these photos when developed, an indication that a spirit may be trying to manifest.

Orbs also appeared on photos taken around the bookshelves, where the investigators also had a feeling of being watched. SJGR also obtained two unexplainable readings on their EMF meters, indicating a fluctuation in the electromagnetic field with no natural sources found that could have caused this.

While the ghost researchers reported drafts, orbs and EMF activity, the spirit life of the library was not overly active the night of their visit. Maybe this is because this little girl's ghost only comes out when children are present, longing to play and learn with the other children. Maybe she is searching for her playmates she left behind, when she was called to an early grave.

The Robins Nest

"The redbreast oft, at evening hours, Shall kindly lend his little aid, With hoary moss, and gathered flowers, To deck the ground where thou art laid."
—William Collins, eighteenth-century English poet, from "Dirge in Cymbeline"

I f you come to Mount Holly to eat and shop, you will likely visit Mill Race Village, a quaint area of old buildings converted into shops and galleries. It is so named for the mill raceway that was dug through the area during the boom of the Industrial Revolution. This waterway led to the Rancocas Creek, which was then navigable enough for boats to take the products of the mills to Philadelphia.

Today, Mill Race Village is an artists' alcove, where those searching for unique items of art, clothing, books and music will find their expectations exceeded by the pleasantly unusual array of products available here. After a busy day of shopping, you may be inclined to stop for refreshment at the Robins Nest, a popular restaurant offering cuisine with a French/American flair that sits at the corner of Washington and White Streets. Patrons flock to Robin Winzinger's outdoor patio and "Crow Bar" during the warmer months for upscale, yet casual drinks and dining along the bank of the Rancocas Creek. Their cozy Victorian dining area inside hosts warm, spirited dining all year long.

The building has been through many transitions before it became the cheerful restaurant it is today. It has been a pool hall, a barbershop, a bakery and in the 1950s it was owned by the military, and mixers were held there. Through the many lives of this building, there were almost always residential accommodations upstairs, until its present reincarnation as the Robins Nest.

Even if you come by yourself to the Robins Nest restaurant, you may not be dining alone.

In the early twentieth century, the building was Mayer's Bakery, owned by Albert Mayer. In *Images of America*, Winzinger and Smith remember that Albert Mayer's shop also had an ice cream fountain where locals gathered for a cool ice cream or soda treat on a hot day in the center of Mount Holly, across from Fountain Square.

The current owner, Robin Winzinger, bought the building in a tax sale in the mid-1980s. The last occupant had been a flower shop, and prior to that it was an RCA appliance store and Robin's grandfather bought his first TV there, she remembered in an interview in October 2007. Robin turned this forsaken building into one of the most popular dining destinations in Burlington County, and her decadent desserts probably have much to do with its success. She has won awards for "Best Desserts" in the Burlington County Reader Choice Award. Robin has restored her restaurant to look much like Albert Mayer's bakery of the 1920s, with the pastry case tempting you as soon as you enter the front door.

Probably the many past lives of the building have left spirits lingering, as Robin has been visited here by ghosts, as have many of her staff and guests. When she first opened the restaurant, she saw a figure of a man at the top of the stairs. He quickly dissipated and she has not seen his tall, dark figure since.

Yet she often hears voices at night on the second floor; she claims that this has been going on since opening this restaurant and continues until this day.

David Karg, who lives over at 111 Garden Street, in a haunted house, remembered in an interview in September 2007 that his grandfather used to live upstairs here when it was a bakery. His name was Harry O'Donald, and he was married to Bessie, a schoolteacher. Harry smoked cigars and played the piano and was very popular around town. Unfortunately, Harry fell victim to Bright's disease and it claimed his life when he was only in his thirties. After his wake, they brought his coffin down the staircase. Could this be the ghost Robin saw at the top of her stairs?

Julie A. Baker-DiCamillo was a manager at the Robins Nest from 2001 to 2004. "It's a scary place," she says. "It is eerie, creepy and haunted." She also does not believe they are friendly ghosts. "You can just sense it; they make themselves known."

Julie even feels that the ghosts at the Robins Nest can be harmful. "It took nerve to go upstairs after closing. I wouldn't go alone unless I was feeling brave." Julie often heard the sound of footsteps coming from upstairs when she knew nobody was there.

It is said that the baker who owned this building had a young daughter who died upstairs while the family was living there. There was an old picture of a little girl upstairs, and Julie said her eyes would follow you. Temperature fluctuations are common upstairs, Julie reports. "I would frequently feel cold, especially in the office." The office is located in the rear of the second floor; it may once have been a bedroom.

On the first floor of the Robins Nest is a cozy, old-fashioned bar with a television hanging behind it. One night late, when the customers were gone, the staff was enjoying some camaraderie in the cozy barroom area. Julie was there, and so were waitresses Amy Morris, Kimberlee Davis-White and others. They were having a good time, joking and laughing, and some were taking pictures of each other. When one of the photos was developed, it showed the face of a man reflected in the television. Kimberlee described the face as similar in style to a young newsboy, with a 1930s-style cap. The TV was not on at the time, and there was no such man at the bar at the Robins Nest that evening, the staff remembered.

There was a particular Tuesday afternoon in the fall of 2003 that Julie will never forget. On Mondays and Tuesdays, the Robins Nest sometimes only serves lunch, so customers are gone by mid-afternoon. On this day, customers had cleared out and the staff had cleaned up and gone home. Julie locked up for the day, as usual. She locked the kitchen door, a door to the outside that has a push bar; once it is locked, it can only be opened from the inside. She then locked the side doors and set the alarm. As she left the building, she saw Donald, one of the dishwashers, outside, so she stopped to chat with him. Donald had a strapping six foot four, muscular frame. Julie and Donald were often the last ones there at night, and even though Donald was a big, physically fit guy, he was no more apt to go up on the second and third floor of the Robins Nest alone at night than Julie was. They have both seen the shadows up there and heard footsteps coming from there when they knew nobody was on the upper floors of the building.

They stood there facing the building, sharing some laughs and conversation, enjoying this golden fall afternoon. The sun was beginning to sink behind the restaurant's frame as the traffic was starting to swell on Washington Street, with people making their way home for the evening after a day's work. Suddenly, the windows on the second floor and the attic started to rattle, and then, bam! The kitchen door flew open! Startled, Julie bolted across the street. Then the alarm went off. Together, they took a few deep breaths and went back in the building, entering through the door of the bar, which is on the side. They cautiously looked around the bar and the dining rooms on the first floor, and then went back to the kitchen and closed that door again, relocked the entire building and reset the alarm. As they walked away from the building, crossing White Street, the kitchen door flew open again. Again, cautiously, they crept back in, checked out the building, found nothing and set the alarm. This time they took a heavy chair and propped it against the outside of the kitchen door.

Julie senses that there is an angry man in the building, and while he has made his presence known to her many times, he does not seem to bother the customers. She says that some of the staff are afraid to go into the basement; she is not afraid of the basement. Julie remarked in an interview in September 2007 that she feels the activity is most apparent on the second floor.

Waitress Amy Morris said in September 2007 that the possibility of disembodied spirits floating around the Robins Nest does not concern her because she does not believe in ghosts. However, she admits she has witnessed, as have most of the other wait staff, that "chocolate milk" comes up on the computer every now and then, and nobody has entered it. "Supposedly a little girl, a little boy and a man died here, and some people think one of the kids is asking for chocolate milk," she says.

Kimberlee has seen the chocolate milk request as well, and she does think that spirits could be haunting the Robins Nest. "It's spooky here, even in the daytime," she says. When she's vacuuming at night, she feels that somebody is watching her.

About twice per month, the Robins Nest hosts tarot card readings and a popular psychic, Vivienne, is on hand to provide cartomancy for interested diners. Robin Winzinger said that Vivienne sees the little girl all the time and has often seen an older woman who appears to be the little girl's grandmother.

All these experiences by staff led to the request to have the Robins Nest investigated by professional paranormal researchers. They reached out to South Jersey Ghost Research (SJGR) to see if they could verify any of things going bump in the day and night as actual spirit activity.

At 6:00 p.m. on February 25, 2000, a clear winter night with temperatures in the mid-thirties, seven investigators from SJGR arrived to see what all the commotion was about at the Robins Nest. Their report includes findings such as objects moving by themselves and strange noises. One investigator encountered a "young female apparition in a yellow dress" and they heard footsteps from the empty attic above them. Orbs dot many pictures taken that evening, and their website reports that their video was showing "numerous anomalies."

SJGR came back to the Robins Nest that summer. Under a full moon, at 9:00 p.m. on July 15, 2000, it was cloudy, in the low seventies, when the eight SJGR investigators arrived, some who had been there in February.

"The two area's [sic] we encountered the majority of the activity on this follow-up investigation were the same as we found on our first trip here," says their official report on their website. Those two areas are the front staircase and the second-floor dining room. Orbs dot photos of the staircase, where Robin saw the male apparition and where Harry O'Donald's coffin had been taken out of the building after his wake.

SJGR's most recent visit to the Robins Nest was on February 10, 2007, a partly cloudy night at twenty-seven degrees. As with previous investigations, the second floor was the most active and where the greater amount of evidence was collected. Five investigators participated in this investigation, and they reported receiving "strong impressions of two spirits." One was a male whom they felt had a connection to the "Old West." The second was a woman from the Victorian era. They report they felt the spirits were benign and in no way harmful to employees or patrons of the Robins Nest. They also collected eleven electronic voice phenomena (EVPs) during this investigation and one positive motion sensor reading, along with energy orbs in photos. The voice was a female voice saying "yes" after one investigator said "hello," according to their website.

On October 11, 2003, a pharmacy across the street from the Robins Nest was completely destroyed by fire. Photos taken that night show orbs flying high above the Robins Nest. Were the spirits trying to escape to safety? Or were they using energy from the heat of the fire to manifest?

Robins Nest is a great restaurant, and now if you go there, you know you will never be dining alone. Maybe you can down a drink at the bar with a

Orbs flying out of the Robins Nest during the 2003 fire. Were the spirits running for their "lives"? *Photo by Rocky D'Entremont.*

"cowboy" who passed through here long ago, shot a few games of pool and now returns looking for a young lady in a yellow dress. Does that poor child ever get her chocolate milk? If you go, won't you treat her to one? She's been waiting so long.

The High Street Grill

A popular dining destination in Mount Holly is the award-winning, Zagat-rated High Street Grill, located at 64 High Street. Owners John and Nancy McDevitt have created a fun, upscale restaurant in this early nineteenth-century building. Their innovative menu and regular wining and dining activities have won them considerable popularity and loyalty of customers, as well as awards and notoriety from *New Jersey Monthly* magazine and *South Jersey Magazine*; if you've dined there, you know why. But it is also a popular spot for those who no longer need to nourish themselves with food or drink. So if it is not John's talent as a gourmet chef or Nancy's hospitality, what brings these visitors to this historic establishment?

"It all started when we were getting ready to open in 2004, and we were here late in the night, sometimes overnight. There was a creepiness to the quiet, like we were not alone, but the one that noticed it the most was our golden retriever, Maggie. She was very spooked about going down or up the steps late at night, and often refused. She had to be literally pushed to go out through certain doors. The most spooky area was the upper dining room," recalls Nancy McDevitt of the early days when they had just bought the building.

Nancy did not feel any spirits that may be lingering were necessarily harboring any ill intent. "I think they were interested in our initial changes and probably wondering, 'What are these people doing?'"

"We may have even ruffled some feathers because we really purged a lot of clutter and leftover junk. We hauled out two dumpsters of trash containing

The brick walls of the High Street Grill contain the energy of spirits from almost two centuries.

all kinds of stuff from three previous restaurant businesses," adds John McDevitt. "Almost thirty years of stuff here that had been untouched."

The third floor of the building is used as an office and storage area. Nancy will often go up there to do administrative work, and while sitting at her computer, she often feels air brush across her back.

Steve Gates worked as a bartender at the High Street Grill when the restaurant first opened, and sometimes his girlfriend at the time, Emily Cohn, would come in to visit while he was finishing work late at night. One night, he was closing up the bar and he felt a presence behind him. He mentioned it to Emily and she swung around quickly and saw what appeared to be an apparition round the corner toward the stairs. Emily also says she has heard the back door open and close when nobody was there, and has sensed someone walking down the stairs. Gates and the McDevitts also noticed the lights going on and off for no reason, as well as always catching shadows in the corners of their eyes and objects falling all by themselves. Bartender David Mongiardo and waiter Brian Strumfels say that these strange occurrences still continue, more than three years after the restaurant opened. They have seen coffee cups and champagne glasses teeter toward the end of shelves and then just fall off, all by themselves. Noises and things falling by themselves are common occurrences here, says Nancy. "These things mostly happen late or when there is quiet in the room."

Customers dining in the second-floor dining room notice lights blinking, breezes coming from out of nowhere and the office door opening by itself. Mongiardo's parents were dining on the second floor one evening. His mother happened to look over toward the third-floor door and saw it opening—not like it just blew open or became unlatched, but as if a person was opening it. The sight made her shudder with chills. McDevitt says this door cannot open like that by itself.

The building has a long history; Nancy says it is built of bricks over 180 years old. Besides serving as several other restaurants before the High Street Grill, this location has also been a pharmacy, a tailor shop and a shoe store in days gone by. Longtime Mount Holly resident Eleanor Rich remembers the building as a shoe store in the 1930s and Natalie Stultz, who lived upstairs with her parents. "It was gorgeous upstairs," recalled Eleanor in a 2005 interview. A building this active for so long is fertile haunting ground and when the feelings of paranormal presence grew in frequency, Nancy thought it was time to find out for sure if her new restaurant was haunted.

On a partly cloudy night with a waxing moon in November 2005, South Jersey Ghost Research arrived at the High Street Grill to do an investigation. Their report on their website states,

> *Due to the brick construction of this building, energy is held within the walls. The history of this building as a bar, pharmacy, shoe store and many other businesses allows for the many different events, emotions in people's lives and the walls contain all of that energy. With all of that history there is a rich amount of information that can be obtained in reference to the spirits within the building.*

The entire SJGR team felt a presence on the third floor, as do the McDevitts. While John and Nancy, as well as many customers dining on the second floor, report the door to the third floor opening by itself and feelings of being watched, two SJGR investigators actually identified the presence they found there as a short female in her late twenties or early thirties, with brown hair. Also in the dining room area, the investigators felt that there were a lot of residual energies present. SJGR also reported a significant amount of positive EMF readings during the investigation throughout the building.

SJGR found activity where a fireplace used to be on second and third floors. Nancy explains that these brick walls "could well be where rooms extended out of the current rooms, possible sites of births, deaths and other human events."

The High Street Grill is one of the officially haunted spots on the Haunted Holly Ghost Tour, and usually the meetings for the ghost tour guides are held at the restaurant to prepare for each tour. The meeting for the July 2007 tour was held in the downstairs tavern area, at a table near the brick wall. A couple of new guides for the tour were former members of a prominent New Jersey paranormal research group, and these two women were seated closest to the wall. As the group discussed the upcoming tour, they explained to the group of tour guides that ghosts are more likely to manifest when they feel that there are more "sensitives" present, i.e., those who believe in ghosts and are open to the signals the spirits are sending out. Therefore, ghosts may manifest during the tour or anytime "sensitives" gather, as they flock to those who seek them.

As the meeting closed, one of the two newcomers, Laurie Miller, a paranormal researcher for five years in the past, reported that she felt like somebody had punched her. "I felt as if I was punched very hard in the collarbone on the right side of my chest. It took the wind out of me for a few seconds," said Laurie of the experience in an interview in January 2008. The only thing behind her was the brick wall, that wall that is believed to contain the energy of almost two hundred years. It is obviously more than residual energy contained there.

Wait staff member Steven Schmidt will never forget the morning he was setting up tables in the tavern area. As he was placing napkins and silverware on a high top, a woman appeared alongside him and asked if they were hiring cocktail waitresses. "I don't think so," he said at first, but then he wondered how she got in, as both the front and back doors were locked. He turned away from her and glanced toward the door, and when he turned back again she was gone, just as quickly as she had appeared. He ran into the kitchen to tell Harry, one of the cooks, as he was the only other person there at the time. Harry hadn't seen her, and knew for sure nobody came through the kitchen door. He tried to calm Steven down, as he was visibly shaken by the visit of this job-seeking apparition.

Although there appears to be considerable ghostly energy in the restaurant, the McDevitts feel the overriding current is positive energy and while the sightings and feelings give them pause, they are not concerned about the ghosts. Said Nancy in October 2007, "We celebrate a lot of happy events here. People get engaged here, celebrate christenings here, we have rehearsal dinners, holiday parties and many other happy times. I think the spirits are probably happy with what the building has become."

Relief Fire Company

"Each separate dying ember wrought its ghost upon the floor."
—Edgar Allan Poe, from "The Raven"

W hen that guy told me to get out, I got out!" recalled Herb Zoll, president of Relief Fire Company. He was telling stories of haunted happenings to visitors on the Haunted Holly Ghost Tour on the evening of Friday, April 13, 2007.

Herb was talking about a spirit he felt one night while working alone in the back office of the firehouse, located on the second floor of this Pine Street building. He had been catching up on some administrative work when a loud, angry voice said, "Get out!" Herb's a big guy, and being a firefighter for many years, he is certainly no sissy. But he did not have to be asked a second time to leave the area.

Relief Fire Company is one of the favorite stops on the ghost walk. Its long history as the oldest continually operating fire department in the United States and its display of memorabilia and pictures of firefighting history dating back to 1752 would be enough to earn this status. But it is also one of the stops richest with paranormal occurrences.

John Grantham has been with Relief since 2000 and is a trustee for the fire company. He notes that Herb is far from being alone in regard to paranormal encounters here. Relief Fire Department's members have had frequent visits by long lost colleagues, both canine and human, some recognized and some not. After numerous experiences by many Relief volunteer firefighters, they finally summoned South Jersey Ghost Research (SJGR) to verify their suspicions. SJGR has come to the firehouse several times and has found positive evidence of paranormal activity each time.

Relief Fire Company, the longest continually operating fire department in the United States, is also long on ghost stories.

As for Herb's antagonist in the second-floor back office, SJGR investigators did produce evidence of ghostly activity in that area, as well as throughout the building. In SJGR's report from an investigation done in September of 2001, one investigator states that she was drawn to the steps, where she took a positive picture showing an orb on the landing stairs, and at that time she also got a man's voice on her recorder that sounded like he may have been saying a name. Orbs dotted many photos taken at the top of the stairs and by the two back rooms on the second floor. Investigators also reported hearing noises in the office. Clearly, Herb is not making this up.

Another grouchy ghost sits in the second-floor meeting room, at the secretary's desk. The firemen know that he's mad and irritated, but they don't know why. While checking out this meeting room, one SJGR investigator heard a voice transmitted over her radio that simply said, "Go." This voice came over her radio only, and was not picked up by any of the radios belonging to the other investigators. It came over twice, according to the investigative report. This investigator stated in her report that maybe the second-floor spirit shuns company because of the meetings and events there. Maybe the gathering of ghost tour participants in this room every Friday the thirteenth to hear the history, the ghost stories and to view the boots, buckets and memorabilia displayed there from firefighting days gone by stirs his ire to an angry tempo. Or maybe it is something more serious, as one SJGR investigator heard a voice relate a possible tale of tragedy. This SJGR investigator came into the room to check out a noise he heard coming from the meeting room while he was in the TV room, also on the second floor, down the hall. While there, he heard a voice that said, "It killed me." He snapped a photo that turned out positive with orbs.

Maybe Herb and other members can take some comfort in a little insight offered by SJGR Director Dave Juliano, who has stated that sometimes voices can be residual energy. In other words, it's like "playing a tape," says Juliano. In an interview on September 21, 2007, Juliano remarked that the energy from an event remains in the area and it can be heard repeatedly, even if the spirit is no longer there.

Consider the planning done by original members of the fire department, who carved out articles of agreement in 1752 that are recounted in Shinn's *The History of Mount Holly*:

> *Upon our first hearing the cry of fire in the night, we will immediately cause two or more lights to be set up in our windows and such our company whose houses may be thought in danger, shall likewise place lights in every room to prevent confusion and that their friends may be able to give them the more speedy and effectual assistance.*

Isn't it very likely that a fireman who would be rushing in to rescue residents in a burning building would be yelling, "Get out!"? The voice would be loud and commanding, just as was the voice heard by Herb Zoll; a fireman trying to quickly evacuate a building would not be friendly and polite. So, another possibility is that Herb's grouchy ghost is residual energy from a fire scene fought long ago.

Another point that Dave explains in his book, *Ghost Research 101*, is that even if it is not residual energy, "don't assume that a spirit is talking to the person who hears them. A spirit or a residual voice can be saying, 'Get out,' but if you don't know who they are talking to, you can't assume that it wants the residents to leave."

Not many who were around the firehouse the day Johnny MacIntosh died will forget that day. Ralph Trout was tidying up the firehouse and racking up the chairs. Suddenly, all the chairs fell off the rack. This could not have happened by itself; members "rack" that one up to Johnny's spirit saying goodbye.

Some spirits enjoy pranks and will do anything for attention. Maybe Johnny's spirit got such a good laugh with that one that he decided to do it again. A separate incident happened soon after Johnny passed, on a night when Ralph was sitting outside with Sue Orangers and a few other members. Suddenly the chairs again fell off the racks, all by themselves, and the heavy fire coats hanging inside the firehouse began to sway. "The wind would not have been able to move them," commented Sue's husband, Ken, Relief's head trustee. But then, there wasn't any wind inside the firehouse anyway.

One day in 2004, Ken Orangers was sitting outside, just in front of the firehouse bay doors, chatting with a few other members. He turned around and looked through the open bay doors and saw a large shadow on the wall. This dark shadow, taller than his own six-foot-plus frame, moved across the wall near the soda machine. Not a soul was in the firehouse at the time (not a living soul, anyway). Photos of the front of the firehouse taken by SJGR show numerous orbs there.

Susan Orangers has been a member of Relief for thirty years. Once heading up the Ladies Auxiliary, she is now the fire department's secretary. She has experienced quite a bit of ghostly activity during her tenure, but nothing stands out in her mind like the posthumous visit from David Bruce. David died in the 1990s, and one night several years after his death, Sue came through the front door of the firehouse into the bay where the trucks are parked. Walking past the hook and ladders, making her way back to the kitchen, she came upon the canteen truck. There, in the driver's seat of the canteen truck, sat David Bruce. There was no doubt to Sue it was him. "Dave was like a brother to me; he was my husband's best friend. He just looked at me and smiled. I was scared of the ghosts at first," says Sue. "But now I know they won't hurt us."

When Fireman Bill Mintz was alive, he always smoked a pipe filled with cherry tobacco in the firehouse. Members often remember Bill, because his tobacco still frequently wafts through the rooms of the building, long after his passing. Jamie Faith Eachus and Dave Juliano of SJGR agree that smells are very common in hauntings, and are sometimes the first sign of a manifestation of a ghost. Cigars and food smells are often experienced when a ghost is manifesting.

One night in 2003, Fireman Nicholas O'Hara was on fire call. He had to use the facilities, so he went into the men's room. Suddenly, he heard the spurt of water starting from a faucet and then the shower came on all by itself. O'Hara peeked around the shower curtain and when he found nobody there, he ran out of the firehouse, across Pine Street and up Church Street to his home as fast as he could, pulling his pants up as he ran. Nick's not the only one to feel a presence in that bathroom. During the September 2001 SJGR investigation, the report log states that one investigator felt very uncomfortable in the men's bathroom, so he also decided to leave.

As with most volunteer fire departments, Relief is always looking for new members to boost its ranks. However, the collective spirits are not always helpful in the fire company's recruitment efforts. In the spring of 2007, a new volunteer came to Relief Fire Department. His aspirations to become a fireman were quickly doused when he walked up the stairs and somebody tapped him on the shoulder. He turned around and, seeing nobody there, he quickly left and never returned. Maybe the old firefighters just feel they are filtering out the recruits they don't feel can cut it!

One night, Ken Orangers was watching TV in the pool room on the second floor. The TV kept going off and on, as did the air conditioning. On other occasions, members report the light at the top of the stairs going on and off for forty-five minutes, always between midnight and one o'clock in the morning. Being an old and historic building, the firehouse is under scrutiny by the township code inspector. Relief Fire Department diligently keeps the electrical system up to snuff, and it is checked regularly by a certified electrician who says there is nothing in the wiring that can be causing the lights to flicker. According to paranormal research groups, pranks with the electrical systems are common hijinks for spirits.

During the September 2001 SJGR investigation, some investigators reported feeling a presence in the poolroom and got multiple pictures dotted with orbs that were taken there. Two investigators reported the sound of pool cues clicking together. When investigator Sue Bove lingered in the poolroom after the other investigators had left, she saw a male apparition peek his head around the doorway of the room. "I got the impression that he was wondering why I hadn't come out of the room with the other investigators," she reported in the SJGR log.

During the SJGR investigation, one investigator was drawn to the steps. She snapped a picture that showed an orb at the top of the landing of the stairs, and she also got a man's voice on her recorder that sounds like he may be saying a name. Other investigators that night report orbs around the stairs and on the second floor. Two investigators reported hearing whispering at the top of the stairs and the EMF detector went off there.

Many firehouses have had fire dogs join their ranks, and Relief is no exception. The last was Jake, who lived a good life and died of old age on July 4, 2001. Molly's death was more tragic. She died in action in 1915. En route from a fire, she fell off the fire truck and was run over. A sad memorial, the graves for both dogs sit side by side, marked by tombstones along the northeast side of the building. Yet the memories and spirits of both dogs remain inside the firehouse. When Jake was alive, he had his own room in the back of the building. Members still hear him howl and growl in the hallway in the back of the firehouse frequently. They hear Molly barking, too. Sue explains that their voices are different, so they know both dogs haunt the building.

SJGR's investigation was only a couple months after Jake's death, and Dave Juliano records in his report that he was drawn to the "dog's room" repeatedly and stated, "I feel there are both human and animal spirits in the building." Several other investigators report being drawn to "the dog's room" and one concurred in the log, "While sitting in the dog's room, I felt something in the room with me."

While Molly's grave is outside the firehouse, her spirit remains inside.

Relief Fire Company originated in Mount Holly as Britannia Fire Company on July 11, 1752. It has had several locations and a few name changes, but it is the oldest continuously active fire company in the United States. It has been known as Relief Fire Company since 1852 and Shinn writes that the cornerstone of its current building on Pine Street was laid on June 18, 1892.

Said SJGR investigator Glenn Huber in his report of the investigation of September 2001, "This firehouse has a lot of neat things about it, and being a firefighter myself, I can appreciate the history of it being the oldest. A lot of great men served in this firehouse, and I got that sense being there this night."

John Grantham said he thinks so many spirits remain at the firehouse because "it's hard to leave. It's one big family. We have about one hundred lifetime members and thirty active members. There are about ten or so of us that are really close. We are always here." Sue Orangers agreed. "Everybody's right here for each other," she said.

Apparently, some have made more than a lifetime commitment.

Thomas Budd House

"A house is never still in darkness to those who listen intently."
–*James Matthew Barrie,* The Little Minister, *1898*

Thomas Budd was a landowner in the early days of Mount Holly. He was involved in many projects vital to the development of Mount Holly, such as the maintenance of the ironworks bridge in 1759, and was also one of the proponents of changing the name of the town from Bridgetown to Mount Holly. In 1765, he was one of the founding fathers of Saint Andrew's Church in Mount Holly and one of the incorporators of the original Bridgetown Library. His brick, colonial-style, two-and-a-half-story home standing at 20 White Street since 1744 is the oldest known dwelling on its original site in town. It remains today almost exactly as it was built centuries ago, except that an adjoining building of similar architecture and built around the same time by his son, Dr. Stacy Budd, was torn down in the 1920s, according to Shinn's *History of Mount Holly*. Some reports claim the Thomas Budd House was used as a headquarters by the colonists during the Battle of Iron Works Hill, also referred to as the Battle of Mount Holly.

Twenty White Street is in the center of what is now known as Mill Race Village, today full of quaint shops and galleries and anchored by the Robins Nest Restaurant. The village is so named because a vital part of its development back in the eighteenth century was the digging of the "mill race," a widening of a segment of the Rancocas Creek that ran through the village and fed the many different mills in the area, providing them with water power and the ability to transport raw materials. Being able to obtain raw materials and power was critical to manufacturing and a thriving economy. Rizzo writes in *Mount Holly, New Jersey*, that Thomas Budd was among the men who were instrumental in digging the millrace that made Mount Holly prosper.

The Thomas Budd house and many of the surrounding buildings of Mill Race Village are quite active with spirit activity, much of which has been validated by South Jersey Ghost Research (SJGR). This cluster of haunted buildings provides several stops on the Haunted Holly Ghost Tour. The Budd house is a neighbor to the Spirit of Christmas and Home Fine Art, and a block from both the Robins Nest and the Bass House, all of which are haunted. Ghosts seem to like this part of town as much as today's shoppers and diners do.

Budd's old house has been the home of several businesses in the past decade. From 1999 through 2005, it was the Candle Garden, owned by Danielle Flagg. After that, it was Uniquely Native, owned by Mary Carty and Cathy "Starfire Woman" Chadwick-Ciccone for two years after the

The Thomas Budd house, the oldest dwelling in town on its original location, is home to at least seven ghosts.

Candle Garden closed. In 2007 it opened as the Bookery, owned by Noel Withers. All owners have reported strange occurrences, as has Mike Geisler, who once rented the apartment upstairs.

On several occasions Mary Carty tried to take pictures of her shop facing Dr. Stacy Budd's side that had been torn down in the 1920s. None of these pictures ever came out, while other pictures from other angles were processed without any problems.

Danielle Flagg experienced seven ghosts while the Candle Garden was in business there. Some of these have also been sighted or felt by the subsequent owners of Uniquely Native, as well as by Geisler. Two ghosts Danielle knew of, one male and one female, stayed pretty much in the crawl space in Mike's apartment. Danielle had the feeling these two were the ghosts of runaway slaves, which was possible since the Underground Railroad passed through Mount Holly. Mike totally disagrees with this identification, or possibly he experienced two completely different ghosts. While both Danielle and Mike sensed excessive anger, pain and fear from these two spirits, Mike got more of a sense that these ghosts were evil. Once he became aware they were ill-spirited, he barricaded the crawl space.

"They were not normal, typical ghosts," he contends, and claims that after other ghost researchers met them, they agreed with him that they were evil. Mike was a member of SJGR when he lived at the Budd house and has always been "sensitive." He still sometimes consults for SJGR and other professional ghost hunters as a psychic. "Not a lot scares me," he says, "I just don't like evil stuff in my house."

All tenants of this building since 1999 have seen the Hessian soldier. He walks loudly with heavy boots, and smells bad. There are several stories floating about concerning why he is here. Some say he was killed here, in this building, during the Battle of Mount Holly. Cathy Chadwick-Ciccone was told he was captured by the colonists and shackled in the cellar for the rape of a young colonial girl. This story claims that the Hessian was killed by the girl's father, bludgeoned through the chest with a bayonet that was taken from the attending guard. Mike and Danielle believe he was a traitor and was bayoneted by his own troops. Mike believes he has firsthand information on this, as the soldier has spoken to him in German. Mike says he saw the Hessian all over the house. He was grouchy and hated company; he even cursed at Mike in German. If Mike had friends over, he would pull the covers off the girls and tickle their feet.

The footfalls of the heavy marching boots, and a foul smell, sometimes like sulfur, were ever present for Uniquely Native owners Carty and Chadwick-Ciccone, too. Mary saw a male apparition one day, a tall dark shadow. He walked from the back office to the back room where she held basket weaving classes. She called to him, but he vanished. Mary and Cathy say that the foul sulfur smell was always at one spot in the doorway between the front and back room whenever the soldier was present. That was where Danielle smelled it, too.

Danielle grew weary of the Hessian and tried to convince him to leave. "I was told that if you talk to spirits and tell them to go, or even think the conversation in your head, they will leave." One day, she was sitting in the office with her back to the basement and she felt someone's presence. She thought about what she had been told.

"I felt funny speaking to someone I wasn't seeing, so I decided to 'think' the ghost away. In my mind, I told him, 'Go to the light, the war is over. It is time you moved on.'" She suddenly felt very warm, then felt as if someone was wrapping his arms around her chest and then squeezing her. She jumped up and ran out of the store. Unfortunately, the only one she convinced to leave was herself, as the Hessian is still there.

There was a spirit in the Budd house that didn't share Cathy's taste in music and decided to do something about it. Being of Lenni Lenape heritage, Cathy enjoyed listening to Native American music while working. The genre varied from traditional, to modern, to ambient, but it was always Indian artists.

> *Very soon, I began to experience a problem with the music. CDs that worked perfectly fine began to skip like crazy, but not all the CDs. Often, the stereo would even shut off, and occasionally, it would turn back on, then off again. This made no sense at all, as the CDs worked fine in my home and car, and the stereo was new. This was witnessed by several customers, as well. I even went so far as to take the stereo home, and play the same CDs, but it never skipped outside of the shop.*

Then one day, Cathy realized there was a pattern. The phenomenon only occurred when vocables were played, never during any other type of music. Cathy explains "vocables" as "native vocalizations, without words, such as 'wey-ya-hey-ya,' often using a high-pitched voice, repeatedly, almost like a wail. This is an older, more traditional type of native music that goes way back, and is still used today."

Realizing this may be what the spirits objected to, she decided to strike up a deal with them. "Okay, you don't like my music. I get it. I probably wouldn't like yours either. We need to come to an agreement," she began to negotiate with them. "I'll make a deal with you. We'll take the days, you can have the nights. I think that's fair." She soon saw a drastic drop in the frequency of the stereo malfunctioning. Then, during the October 13,

2006 Haunted Holly Ghost Tour, she related the experience to a group of ghost tour participants. As if on cue, the stereo shut off, as witnessed by approximately thirty people. Several people investigated to be sure there was no trickery. Cathy's hands remained on the countertop at all times. The stereo shared an electric outlet with a cable strip that had three lamps plugged into it, and they were unaffected.

Danielle also felt the presence of an old woman ghost who stayed in one section of the basement. Danielle always felt sadness if she went down there. The old woman caused no harm, only sadness. "But one part of the basement you don't want to be in is where the ghost of the groundskeeper stayed. You actually feel him telling you to get out," says Danielle.

Danielle's friend, Diane, was very skeptical of the ghost stories she heard from her friend, until the day she was in the basement helping Danielle with inventory. They were counting candles, laughing and talking, and then… they both heard footsteps. They stopped their work, stood up and listened. Next came a loud crash! Then a box from the other side of the room came flying at them, as if someone had hurled it straight toward them. Terrified, they ran up the stairs. Nobody else had been down there—no other live person, anyway. Diane no longer doubted the stories Danielle told of the ghosts in the Budd house, or the nastiness of the former groundskeeper.

Danielle has actually seen the groundskeeper's ghost in the basement. "He's very nasty. He kind of looks like an emaciated Jerry Garcia, with funky teeth and bulging eyes."

Cathy and Mary felt the presence of the groundskeeper too, and often attributed another foul smell to him, one of sweat, or maybe like stinky socks. But one story of the groundskeeper Cathy describes as "the most amazing experience I have ever had in my life."

It occurred on an unbearably hot summer day in 2006. It was late in the afternoon, and as Cathy recalls this humid day drawing to a close, she tells of harvesting herbs she grew on the back porch of Uniquely Native.

After we closed up the shop, I was alone, and my intention was to harvest the herbs for drying, to package and sell in the shop. I grew basil, Greek oregano, lemon thyme and common sage, also known as kitchen sage and garden sage. I began cutting the herbs, one variety at a time, bringing them into the shop, and spreading them in baskets to dry. The last one I brought in was the sage.

I was in the workshop, bundling and tying the sage to dry, when I began to feel an uncomfortable presence about me. I tried to convince myself I was imagining things, but was unable to shake the feeling. The presence began to grow stronger, and I felt very unwelcome in my own shop, even

> *threatened. So, as is my custom, I spoke to the spirit, recognizing it was a very angry, male presence. I told him, "I know I told you we would take the days, and you could have the nights, but I have work to do. I don't mean to disrespect you, and will not be very long."*

Trying to hurry and finish her work, the presence grew stronger and as Cathy grew increasingly nervous, she also began to experience physical changes.

> *My breath quickened, my pulse raced, and I began perspire. The hair on the back of my neck and arms stood up, my thighs tingled, my left hand and arm swelled. I felt cool and clammy, even though the temperature was near or above ninety. I had a strong sense that what I was doing was wrong, but I could not understand it. I decided I'd had enough, and I put the sage in a basket in the back room and hurried out the back door.*

She put her key in the deadbolt to lock the door, but the key would not turn. This had never happened before. She could not leave the store unlocked, and she could not get her key out of the door. As she continued to struggle with the lock, her anxiety grew in direct proportion to the increasing presence she felt. She felt she had done something wrong, but did not know what it was. She spoke out loud, "I'm sorry, what did I do? I don't understand." Then she felt a firm grip squeeze the back of her neck, though there was no pain. She began to cry out of fear, saying repeatedly, "I'm sorry, I'm sorry." She felt the grip released from her neck, so she ran off the porch to the driveway and called Mary, who lived nearby.

Knowing that Cathy would not be so upset over something trivial, Mary was worried and came right over. Meanwhile, Cathy went back to try the lock again. Still, it would not turn. Finally, she released her grip on the key and, it "popped" out of the lock, almost as if it were pushed out from the inside. The key did not drop straight down to the floor. It "jumped" about a foot straight out and then fell to the mat below. Almost immediately, there was a loud crash. Although very frightened, Cathy tried but was unable to open the door. A heavy object was blocking the door, preventing it from opening.

Mary and her son Steven arrived. Shaking, Cathy told them about her experience, while Steven pushed and shoved, trying to get the door open. He was able to open it just enough to squeeze through. Upon entering, he found that what was blocking the door were two six-foot folding tables that had been bungee corded to another door, which was nailed shut. These large, heavy tables had come crashing down and, along with other items, were wedged between a seven-foot bookcase and the door they were barricading. "Steven picked up the tables and I was able to enter. The cords had not snapped or frayed in any way. It was as if they had been released by some unseen force."

Steven checked out the front rooms, and things seemed fine there. But they both noticed a "staleness" to the air, and it seemed almost vacuum-like. They went toward the back room, and as they entered it, they both began to experience physical changes to their bodies. "We felt cooler, tingly; the hair on the back of our necks and arms stood up, and breathing became uncomfortable. We hurriedly turned, locked the door and left," recalls Cathy.

The next day, Steven told Cathy he was convinced these manifestations had something to do with the sage. Cathy says,

> I was confused. I sold dry, packaged sage in the shop, and as a Lenape Indian, I frequently practiced a Native American purification ritual called "smudging," both inside and outside the house, using smoldering desert sage, or white sage. The intention is to banish negativity, and for space clearing and prayer. I could not understand why the sage would cause such offense now, after so much time.

Steven, who is knowledgeable in herbs and folklore, told her that throughout history, certain characteristics were often attributed to herbs and flowers. He told her that some of his research has shown that during colonial times, people believed "the wife rules when sage grows vigorously in the garden." Cathy herself has since done research that supports this belief, which the colonials brought with them from England. Cathy surmised from her experience, Steven's knowledge and her own research that the groundskeeper was undisturbed by the "foreign" white and desert sage, but took great offense to the garden sage, so she promptly took it out of the shop.

There is another woman who is seen in the Budd house, a colonial woman with her hair pulled up in a chignon and wearing a long, blue dress. She has been seen by Danielle, Mike, Mary and Cathy. One day, Danielle was standing at the counter in the front room of the store, looking into the back room. On the opposite wall is an old fireplace mantel. Danielle saw this woman walk toward that mantel and disappear. During the July 13, 2007 Haunted Holly Ghost Tour, several members of one tour group tried to snap a photo of this mantel. None of their cameras would work. The cameras had worked for pictures at previous stops and they worked for pictures taken later, but none were able to take a picture of where this ghost had appeared and vanished.

Mary and Cathy experienced this same ghost soon after they opened Uniquely Native. "A female apparition glided right past me, not three feet away, and dissolved into the front door," recalls Cathy. "All the while, her left arm was outstretched, as if she was reaching for something. I spoke to her repeatedly, saying, 'I see you. Do you see me?' I don't believe she did." Mike believes that this is the only ghost in the building who is residual energy because she would never interact with anybody. He believes all the others are interactive spirits.

A very interactive spirit is the little boy ghost who Mike and Danielle have both seen. It is reported that a little boy died of an illness in the house. Maybe he was one of Dr. Budd's patients. This little boy wants to play. Mike would see him running around in circles and playing tricks, a seemingly happy child. Danielle felt him following her around too. She kept a fountain running in her candle shop that produced a steady stream of water. One day, she heard it make an unusual splash. When she heard it the second time, she went over to check it out. Looking at the fountain, she saw a break in the water, as if somebody was putting their finger in it; all you could see was an unexplainable break in the running water. She believes it was the ghost of the little boy playing with the water in the fountain.

Random unexplainable happenings occur frequently in this building marking the oldest residence in Mount Holly. Danielle tells of candles lighting by themselves and she and the others tell of objects moving. "I just dealt with it," says Danielle. "There was no harm done; I just felt uncomfortable."

Cathy laughs,

> *Things seemed to "disappear" in the Budd house, only to "reappear" in the most unusual of places. Often, I would find an object moved to another room, strategically placed, as if it were put there for...decoration? Occasionally, I would open in the morning, and there would be one broken candle and glass in the front room, always several feet from where it should, logically, have fallen.*

Cathy and Mary often used a large, old, heavy hammer to gently tap the front bolt open when the old door swelled and the bolt jammed in high humidity. This hammer was kept behind the trashcan at the point of sale. When Cathy went to look for it one evening, it was not in its usual place. She later found it in the bathroom. While Cathy attempted to place the blame on Mary, she could not because the shop was packed with Mary's basket weaving class. All students knew Mary was very busy with the class and attested to her innocence.

Another playful spirit inhabiting Mike's apartment upstairs was a little gray tabby cat. Mike is the only one of these tenants to be acquainted with this spirit, perhaps because he stayed in Mike's apartment. Kitty ghost would knock things off the TV. In true feline fashion, if a skeptical friend was over, Kitty would knock candles off the TV, making sure they would land at the skeptic's feet.

Once during the fall of 2006, Cathy returned to the shop after closing with her husband to get something she had left behind. After the incident that summer, she no longer went there alone late at night. When they were both inside, yet in different areas of the shop, Sal called to her, "Cat, quick, come 'ere! Do you hear that?"

Becoming silent, they heard what Sal described as a section of tenor drums. It repeated slowly and lasted two to three minutes. A highly accomplished drummer and teacher with over thirty years' experience, Sal identified the drum pattern as a colonial military cadence.

"The sound seemed to be 'suspended' in midair in the front room of the shop," says Cathy. They looked outside and listened for noise upstairs, but could find no source for the drumbeat. Sal, excited, but nervous, could scarcely believe what he was hearing, even though he was familiar with and believed Cathy's tales of spirit activity in the shop. Later, Sal confided to Cathy that it reminded him of a "march to the gallows."

After all this time, "we can still call up that rhythm in our minds. Dum… dum…dum, da-da-da-da-dum, over and over again."

When Mike Geisler lived at the Thomas Budd house, he participated in SJGR's two investigations of the property, the first in December of 2001 and the next the following February. While most reports of the investigators these two evenings document photos with orbs, substantial temperature fluctuations, feelings of being watched or overcome with nausea or difficulty breathing, it is very interesting that many of the SJGR reports concur with the experiences of those who worked or lived here. Several investigators report being followed around by a little boy; one even sensed that he was making faces at her. Using copper rods, SJGR investigators also located the spirit of a dominant male. Further investigation revealed this male spirit was also shadowed by a female spirit. Could the male be the Hessian soldier? Or the groundskeeper? Could the female be the colonial woman or the sad woman in the basement?

Several investigators experienced the ghosts in the crawl space Mike had met, and they agree with him that they are unsavory characters. Here are some comments from their individual reports of the February 2002 investigation:

At 11:22 pm I was in the Bathroom Crawl space sitting in the back closet when I felt 2 distinct presences, I felt one right in front of me which gave me the feeling that that presence was a small girl that was scared. I also got a feeling that, that presence felt trapped. The other presence I felt above me was not nice at all, and I felt like this presence was very, very angry, I felt like this presence was hovering over me and I started to feel like I was suffocating and I had to leave the area and go outside for some fresh air…I have never experienced anything like this before, the feelings that I was getting from these 2 distinct presences was unforgettable.

…Based on the strong feelings I got, coupled with the EMF readings, I feel that the blue room, Mike's room, and the crawl space are the most active areas of the house. However, I think that whatever is in the crawlspace is evil.

…took photo (10:46) showing a cluster of orbs in the small back section of the closet. I felt that someone was hiding from all of us in there.

Thomas Budd, wealthy and active in the community, certainly left a legacy for Mount Holly. But the mysterious hauntings in his old house were probably not what he intended to leave behind.

The Spirit of Christmas

"'It's Christmas Day!' said Scrooge to himself. 'I haven't missed it. The Spirits have done it all in one night. They can do anything they like. Of course they can. Of course they can.'"
—Charles Dickens, A Christmas Carol

The dawn of the new millennium found Jo Colino searching for a location to open her new business. Jo is an artist and has worked with acrylics, clay and mixed media. She also worked for a couple of decades as an art consultant for major corporations, decorating their office and conference room walls with art from all over the world. Now she was shifting gears in her life, or maybe we should say changing palettes, and dreamed of owning a year-round Christmas store. She wanted to carry unique ornaments, decorations and cards for Christmas and other major holidays. It would not be like those chain stores with franchises all over the country selling the same items everywhere to everyone, so being enclosed in a mall or any type of shopping center would not suit the quaint, old-fashioned atmosphere of the shop she had in mind. She was hunting for a shop that stood as a single building, among other shops selling uncommon items. Jo feared she may not be able to afford such an exceptional location.

Jo even consulted a medium in her search to find her ideal location. The medium assured her she would find it, and she would know right away when she did. The medium said, "You are going to go to someplace very old. I will give you two initials: MH." Later during her reading, the medium also advised her that just the initial "H" would also be important. She also told Jo that she would hear church bells.

One day Jo was talking to a fellow artist and in their conversation, Jo relayed to her friend her dreams for her new Christmas shop and the uniquely artistic and special type of location she desired for her business. The friend said, "You are describing Mill Race Village in Mount Holly," to which Jo replied "Where's that?"

So one afternoon, Jo left her home in Cherry Hill and drove north on I-295 to the Mount Holly exit. She drove past the mansions and lawyers' offices on High Street, through the business district and across Washington Street into the Mill Race Village section. She parked her car and got out to walk around. "Seeing the quaint shops and galleries, the ducks swimming in the stream, I knew right away this is where I was supposed to be," she says of her first visit to Mount Holly. Then the bells of Saint Andrew's Church chimed, as they do every hour, and Jo remembered the seer's prediction of hearing church bells. She thought about the initials and realized the "MH" was Mount Holly. But what was the "H"?

As Jo walked around Mill Race Village, her spirits began to sink as she saw no vacancies. She stopped to talk to some of the shopkeepers chatting outside. She told them of her quest and her disappointment in finding no vacancy for her to set up her business. She felt her heart pound as they told her that the shop across the street, Old Dog Antiques, would soon be closing. She asked who she could see immediately to grab the vacancy before it went to someone else. She was directed to Heidi Winzinger. She thanked them and went about to find Heidi. She stopped in her tracks at the thought of the fortuneteller's other "H": Heidi. Jo felt her fate was sealed.

Jo opened Spirit of Christmas at 14 White Street, the former home of Michael Ernest, in 2001. Ernest, a Quaker and an animal husbandman, supposedly built his home in 1775, according to the plaque hanging outside. However, the house may have been built earlier, as the deed shows that Mr. Ernest's wife, Ann Bennett, apparently inherited the property from her brother, Thomas Bennett of Philadelphia. The only change since the early construction of this structure is that a covered porch has been added, according to the Daughters of the American Revolution's *Historic Mount Holly, New Jersey*. Jo has looked for Michael Ernest's grave in the cemetery of the Mount Holly Friends, but many headstones from the early 1800s and before are too worn to read.

Two months before Jo opened for business at Spirit of Christmas, Mildred Sherman moved out of the upstairs apartment. This address had been Mildred's family's home for years; after the building was sold, Mildred stayed there, renting the upstairs apartment. Although Mildred was gone and Jo had not met her, Jo felt that the positive energy from Mildred remained and pervaded the atmosphere of Spirit of Christmas. She hoped to somehow find Mildred or someone that knew her so she could meet her.

One afternoon in 2002, Jo was standing at the front room of her shop behind the cash register, talking to Kelly, one of her staff. Kelly was across this

The spirits in this Christmas Shop say "humbug!" to leaving this enchanting store.

room, which is always crammed tighter than Santa's sleigh early on Christmas Eve with delicate ornaments, music boxes, snowmen and other items that practically shout tidings of good cheer to those that enter. Suddenly, in the foyer appeared a woman, about five feet, six inches tall, dressed in a 1940s-style dress patterned with dark and light gray scrolls. Her salt-and-pepper hair that seemed to match the colors of her dress was pulled away from her face…or where there should be a face. The woman had no face! "She was there, and then she was gone," recalls Jo of the visit. "I felt I just saw the essence of her, and felt that she very much wanted me to see her." Kelly very much did not want to see the apparition, and ran outside, terrified.

About a year had gone by since opening Spirit of Christmas and Jo still thought about Mildred and felt that her energy continued to pervade the shop. Then one afternoon in 2002, a young woman entered Spirit of Christmas. She introduced herself to Jo as Bonnie and said that she and her sister, Nancy, used to come here frequently because their aunt had lived upstairs, until just a year or so ago. Jo said to Bonnie, "I have been waiting for you."

Bonnie told Jo that Mildred still lived nearby, in a nursing home on Richmond Avenue in Lumberton, just on the edge of Mount Holly. Jo asked if it would be all right for her to visit Mildred. Bonnie said, "She'd come here and get you herself if she could!"

Jo eagerly made plans to finally meet the woman whose family had lived in the building for so many years. Before making the visit, she wrapped gifts from her shop to take to Mildred. Their visit lasted several hours and they became friends. Mildred told Jo that she planted the dogwood tree that now grows behind the shop and how she longed to see it in bloom again. The next time Jo visited, she "gave the tree a haircut" and wrapped the boughs in beautiful ribbons and took them to Mildred.

Jo would make many visits to Mildred over the next four years. She often brought her gifts, sometimes items from her shop, but it was the dogwood branches from the tree behind her former beloved home that Mildred loved the most. Jo felt that Mildred gave her the best gift by telling her the stories of the past life of her Christmas shop. The building had been home to a happy family for many years. There, Mildred's family would gather for holidays and celebrations; children and laughter filled the rooms that are now filled with bright holiday decorations.

One day, in May of 2006, Jo prepared to visit Mildred and gathered the branches from the dogwood tree out back. It was the tree's time to show off, in perfect bloom that time of the year; Jo admired the white, fragrant blossoms bursting with pink centers as she selected the stems for Mildred's bouquet and the warm spring breeze tickled the branches. Just as she was about to leave, Jo got a call from Bonnie telling her that Mildred had passed. Deeply saddened, Jo saved the dogwood bouquet for Mildred's viewing the next evening. She laid the branches down next to Mildred, as she said her goodbye to the woman who lived many of her ninety-six years in the building where Jo spends much of her life today. Mildred was laid to rest with the branches from her dogwood tree next to her in her casket. Although gone, Jo still feels to this day the strong bond she had with Mildred.

Jo also feels a presence in the basement of her shop, which she uses for storage. One October evening in 2003, Jo summoned Jamie Faith Eachus, assistant director of South Jersey Ghost Research (SJGR), who is also a medium, to come over to Spirit of Christmas and check it out. Jamie was in Mount Holly with SJGR manning an information booth on ghost research at Mount Holly's annual Halloween festival, then called the Witches' Ball. Using only her psychic powers and not any of SJGR's professional equipment, Jamie says she did "pick up on" a man in the basement who said he had died there, possibly from a heart attack. Jo is not afraid down in the basement, but is not particularly comfortable there in his presence, either. However, he has never done her any harm.

Jo feels the spirits of Christmas and other good times past have led her to her location and remain there with her today. Her warm welcome to those who enter her shop and her sparkling inventory have certainly brought spirit to many of her customers' Christmases in the present. The woman in the foyer and the man in the basement are probably just a few of the spirit energies in this store. Jo looks forward to a happy future of continuing her Christmas shop in Mount Holly. Maybe it is the happy times of family and laughter, present in this building for centuries, that make these spirits loathe to leave. Or is it the happy season Jo celebrates all year long that makes her feel the positive energy of spirits in this shop? Humbug to those who feel otherwise.

Mount Holly Friends Meeting House

*"To turn all we possess into the channel of universal love
becomes the business of our lives."*
–John Woolman, Mount Holly Meeting of Friends

T here is no way to peace; peace is the way," proclaimed a banner
that flew for many months recently outside the Mount Holly Friends
Meeting House. While this recent decoration was most likely making a
statement on the war with Iraq, the early days of this historic building also
found it embroiled in the conflict of war at that time. Opposition to war is
probably one of the best-known tenets of the Quaker doctrine, and John
Woolman, one of the key organizers of the Friends in the early days of
Mount Holly, was one of the most outspoken opponents to war, slavery and
other controversial and ethical topics of his time.

The Mount Holly Friends Meeting House was built in 1775. It was
actually the third site for this congregation; the first was built in 1716 at
the foot of the northern slope of the Mount near Woodpecker Lane and
the second was on Mill Street near John Woolman's tailor shop. Ellis Derry
writes in *Old and Historic Churches of New Jersey*,

> *The Burlington Monthly Meeting authorized the building of the Friends
> Meeting House on land purchased from John Brainerd at the corner of
> Main and Garden Streets. The foundation was built of ironstone from a
> quarry on the South Branch of the Rancocas River. Joel Fenton's brick-
> works in Burlington furnished the bricks, the lumber was rough-sawn by a
> gate mill, the planing was done by hand, the mouldings were worked out of
> solid lumber and the frames and windows were all constructed on site.*

In the early days, the lower portion of High Street was known as Main Street. The meetinghouse still stands today at the corner of Garden and High Street, in the center of Mount Holly. And although Woolman and his fellow Quakers, who composed about half of the early population of New Jersey, wanted no more than to live in peace, they found their new house of worship embroiled in the American Revolution in 1776 and temporarily housing the state legislature a few years later.

During the Battle of Iron Works Hill, which was fought in Mount Holly practically in front of the Friends Meeting House and led to Washington's victory in Trenton, the Hessians destroyed our ironworks and ransacked our town. Looting buildings and homes and drinking all the cider and beer they could find, the Hessians also stole cattle from the colonists and set up the Friends Meeting House as a slaughterhouse, according to Rizzo's *Mount Holly*. Some of the benches here show the marks from cleavers used to cut the meat and some pillars sport rope marks from hanging and hauling provisions.

In the mid-nineteenth century, the population of Friends grew and it was necessary to raise the roof and add a gallery, thus increasing the seating capacity by 50 percent. The present iron fence was erected in 1896. The

The Friends Meeting House found itself embroiled in battle and today is haunted by peaceful ghosts.

meetinghouse also housed a school beginning in 1893, but only for a few years. The horse sheds on the grounds were removed in the 1930s due to lack of use, writes Derry in *Old and Historic Churches*. The burial grounds are on site and near the Garden Street fence lies the grave of Sarah Woolman, John's wife, as documented by the DAR. Perinchief writes in *History of Cemeteries in Burlington County, New Jersey*, that she died of smallpox while on a visit to England.

Based on South Jersey Ghost Research (SJGR) investigation logs, it appears that some parishioners and caretakers may have been concerned by strange events that happened at the meetinghouse, and that some felt a presence during prayer meetings. Twelve SJGR investigators showed up to detect the ghostly activity one balmy night in August of 2001, under the light of a full moon.

"I had a sense of female energy on the first floor…throughout the time I was on the first floor," reported one SJGR investigator in his log.

Investigators searched the entire building, as well as the grounds and the adjoining cemetery. "I felt there was a lot of activity in the cemetery but unfortunately conditions were not right for me to get evidence to that. The air in the house was unusually still. Similar to if everyone was holding their breath. It made me feel as if we were the ones being observed not the other way around," reported investigator Laurie Miller.

"I was almost immediately drawn to the back stairs which led down to the first floor. I felt like I wasn't alone," said one investigator as she took a picture of two orbs on the stairs. Orbs also appeared in pictures of the stairs, in the kitchen and in the main room of the second floor over the balcony.

Investigators picked up sounds on tape, particularly a female voice at one point saying, "Christine, Christine," one saying, "Hello," and another saying, "Get out here." Another reported that he heard a male saying, "Interactive."

One investigator got the feeling a spirit was following SJGR Director Dave Juliano and photographed an orb over his chest. Yet Juliano believes that it is mostly residual energy at the Friends Meeting House. That is, the energy of past spirits, events and emotions are retained in the building, rather than active or earthbound spirits. "There are no spirits there, except maybe on the second floor, where the motion detectors went off," contends Juliano. "What we found was a lot of residual energy. This is energy imprinted in the environment. It was like a theater of emotions. The voices heard there are residual energy; they will not interact. It is like playing a tape; it doesn't change."

Investigator Anne Palagruto agreed with Juliano about the residual energy, but can definitely describe the spirits she met there that night. She reports in her log, "I felt a very young woman or girl in the back room, a chubby older man with white hair in a ponytail and a blue suit near the bookcase on the second floor on the top of the stairs in the front. I feel that all this is residual energy."

Investigator Sue Bove told of her experience of the night in her report:

> *I felt the strongest presence of spirits on the 2nd floor of this building. I felt the 12 year old girl who I believe hung around for a while checking us out. I also believe that she was keeping close to our guide, perhaps because she was familiar to her. I think that's why I kept getting pics of our guide showing anomalies near her. I also felt brief periods on the main floor of this building of a presence near me and got + pics when this occurred. Despite the history of this building, I felt a very warm and welcoming feeling in all areas, but especially on the 2nd floor in classroom section. I was very drawn to the back steps on this floor and felt compelled to sit there. Many + pics were taken by myself and other investigators in this area. Overall, I simply loved this very historic building and look forward to conducting further research here. My great thanks to the Friends members who hung out with us and supplied us with some great historical facts.*

Investigator Deb Nielsen summed up that investigation by writing in her report, "I would say, judging by the activity and by what I was able to feel, there are at least 2 spirits in the house. I would say that they were very interested and curious in what we were doing and that they are friendly and show no negativity or malicious intent."

It appears that the ghosts of the Friends Meeting House, be they residual energy, earthbound spirits or both, adhere to the peaceful ways of the Quakers. The Hessians appear to have moved to other sites in Mount Holly, respecting the ideology of the Quakers and their peaceful ways.

Hosting Ghosts

Hauntings in Mount Holly Homes

"If a man harbors any sort of fear…it makes him landlord to a ghost."
–Lloyd C. Douglas

THE JEMIMA SHINN-LIPPINCOTT HOUSE

In late August of 2003, Dave moved into the old Jemima Shinn-Lippincott house on Buttonwood Street, which once also housed the Buttonwood School and stands a few doors down from the old Mount Holly Dairy. It was a steamy August night and Dave was exhausted from unpacking and dragging boxes up and down the stairs. To add to his weariness, there were electrical problems in the house and the only room that would support an air conditioner was the back bedroom, on the second floor. He decided that was the logical room in which to spend the first night in his new home, and after washing up, he collapsed face down in bed and fell asleep. At 3:00 a.m., he awoke abruptly as someone was forcefully rubbing their hands down the entire length of the back of his body.

"It woke me right out of my sleep. I know I wasn't dreaming because I got up and looked at my watch and it was 3:00 a.m. I jumped out of bed and just started reciting the Lord's Prayer over and over. Then I got back in bed but could not sleep for the rest of the night. I left the bedroom at the crack of dawn."

The next night, he sat on the sofa in his new living room, waiting for clothes to finish in the dryer and pondering the placement of furniture in the room. Suddenly, he felt a hand firmly grasp and shake his shoulder. At that moment, he heard the buzzer on the dryer go off.

"That's it!" he screamed at the spirits as he jumped off the sofa. "This isn't supposed to happen! You aren't supposed to be here!" He paced the hardwood floors of the living room, shouted at the spirits and cursed the former owner, who had sworn the house was not haunted. What was he to do now? He thought, he cursed, he paced some more. He had so many plans for this historic home, so many ideas for its restoration. He had no plans for cohabitating with spirits, so he must figure out how to handle this. He was already sweating from the August heat, and now the thoughts clashing in his mind about the spirits pervading his home made this heavy blanket of humidity close in around him like a suffocating shroud over his head. An idea came to him: he decided to make a deal with the ghosts. What did he have to lose?

"Spirits!" he beckoned, sweat dripping down his face and neck. He did not know if they were still present, if they would be interested in his bargain or if they were sneering and hovering impatiently, ready to flaunt their displeasure at his offering as well as to his invasion into their domain. Trying to act in good faith and appease the spirits, he offered them the back bedroom, where they had visited him the first night. They could have that room if they would just leave him alone in the rest of the house.

The spirits must have considered Dave's offer a reasonable compromise. They have not physically touched him since that stifling August night, yet he feels their presence and they still make themselves known, perhaps challenging him to renege on his deal. Orbs do occasionally show up in photos taken in the living room, the room where he had his shoulder shaken, and about once a month he is woken by loud noises, always at 3:00 a.m.

Dave has converted the shambled house he bought in 2003 into an elegant home, restored to period detail, a favorite on Mount Holly's Holiday House Tour. Maybe the spirits are pleased with the elaborate renovations and the care he gives the home they share. Dave's sister thinks that maybe the numerous portraits he has purchased from art galleries are keeping the spirits at bay and their activities to a minimum. Well, not completely. One evening in August 2007, almost four years to the night after he moved in, he was sitting on his bed and a reed chair placed across the room began to squeak; no one was near it. His Airedale, Emma, stood at the doorway, ears up, refusing to take her usual place at her master's side; she would not cross the threshold.

And that room he gave the ghosts…it is right down the hall. Emma often stands at the door. She will not enter the room; she just stares up at the ceiling.

THE SAMUEL CARR HOUSE

At 111 Garden Street sits the home of David Karg, an artist. In pre–Revolutionary War years, this home lacked the elegance of the library and living room now spanning the front of the house. The original exterior was clapboard over a frame of brick and mortar. The cellar floor was dirt, and remains so. The house boasts nine working fireplaces, but none is as spectacular as the Inglenook fireplace in the kitchen, which is immense, framed in carved concrete over a metal and wood frame. This hearth is a cozy resting place for Karg; he keeps a chair within the fireplace frame itself, in front of the fire. Just as his colonial forefathers warmed themselves inside their kitchen fireplaces, Dave often relaxes there, taking the chill out of crisp Mount Holly winter evenings. With the crackling fire at his side and a pot of clove and cinnamon–infused tea nearby, the spice of his creativity and imagination pervades the air here, as does the aroma of the tea. Dave is fond of telling folks that this massive fireplace was the only structure left standing after the Hessians stormed Mount Holly during the American Revolution. But, in truth, that is one of his inventive tales. The extraordinarily massive fireplace is one of Dave's own artistic masterpieces, and one of the many imaginative touches he has added to this distinctive Garden Street home.

In 1775, Samuel Carr and his family came to Mount Holly from Egg Harbor and purchased 111 Garden Street, a small English frame house at the time. The DAR's *Historic Mount Holly, New Jersey*, notes that Samuel Carr owned the ironworks on Pine Street and descended from a lineage of Swedish explorers. Settling in Mount Holly, the Carrs joined the Friends and were instrumental in establishing the Friends' meetings in this town and, eventually, the Friends Meeting House down the street on the corner of Garden and what is now High Street. The Carrs began the evolution of this house by adding the two rooms on the front of the house.

A plaque in front of the house tells of the tragedy in the Carr family that happened on Halloween of 1778. Abigail Carr was waiting for her husband with a kettle of warm tea on the fire. At that same time, Samuel Carr was making his way home along Burlington Road. It was a dark stormy evening, and Carr was struck by a bolt of lightning that claimed his life. When his wife heard the news, she screamed so loudly that she shattered the window glass before falling into a deep recline. She never recovered. She stayed in a perpetual state of mourning, crying throughout the house. A year later, on the anniversary of her husband's death, she died of a broken heart.

The owners succeeding the Carrs, in the 1800s, added an addition on the side of the house. Later in that century, the front addition was covered with stucco, emulating Greek Revival architecture, en vogue with the trend of the time, and it was painted to look like stone. Near the end of the 1800s, the building became a girls' school.

At the turn of the nineteenth century, 111 Garden Street bloomed into grandeur, adorned with lush Victorian gardens. Its features of tulips and bamboo earned it the recognition of one of the great gardens of the United States. The building was once a meeting place for the Mount Holly Garden Club. A woman was often photographed resting on a bench on the front porch, framed by the horticultural masterpiece.

Dave Karg was born and raised in Mount Holly, but later moved to Philadelphia to study and pursue his work in the arts. When his parents became ill in the early 2000s, he moved back to Mount Holly to be near them, and this unusual house struck a chord with his creative nature, so he purchased it for his home. Dave's contributions to the home's continual evolution have been mostly true to the colonial or Victorian period, with his own unique embellishments. Like the Victorians, he loves Christmas trees

Gargoyles and a heavy gate guard the haunted old Samuel Carr house.

and several decorate the lavish rooms of his home all year long. Also, as those in these earlier periods did, Dave keeps company with mannequins, and a handsome male mannequin stands ready to guide you from the library to the music room.

While Dave lives an art-filled life, he feels that his artistic life has been diminished by the loss of his twin brother, Fred, who was also an artist. They often painted in tandem, "like Currier and Ives…I would start a painting and he would finish. When I lost him, I finally realized what it meant to be a twin." On the day Fred passed, Dave left his beloved brother's deathbed and walked out into the corridor of the hospital to see the nurse. He felt his chest thrust forward and the jolt set him back. At that point, he knew the spirit of his twin brother had left his own body.

Dave enjoys living solitaire, but at times he knows he is not completely alone. Besides his black cat, Mr. Franklin, he also shares his home with spirits from the past. Sometimes as he walks the hallways of his historic home, the floorboards move, *after* he has passed by. At night, he has felt someone pushing on his bed. Another time, the spirits became more aggressive. Dave felt a presence hover over his body, almost suffocating him. He couldn't move and he had difficulty breathing.

Downstairs in the basement, a creepy low-ceiling room with a dirt floor and plenty of spider webs, Dave feels he is being watched. While he doesn't feel it is someone with malevolent intent, he has made the decision not to go down there unless absolutely necessary. His girlfriend does not like to stay at the house at all because of the presence of spirits.

Upstairs, Dave has seen a partial apparition: the shadow of a half man. Could this be the spirit of a young man who died next door on the third floor? The next-door neighbor has also sensed this spirit lingering.

Dave's sister is clairvoyant and has always sensed a presence when visiting her brother's home. When the family gathers in his music room and Dave entertains at his player piano, his sister often sees orbs surround Dave as he plays. Perhaps it is the manifestation of the Victorian woman of the garden, coming in from her bench on the porch, lured by the old-time rhythms Dave loves to play? Or maybe it is the spirit of Dave's grandfather, who was a composer and often played himself, a popular Mount Holly musician.

Using an Angel Board, Dave's sister has summoned the spirits of their brother, father and grandfather to the home, and they have been felt there. Dave's brother and father have spoken to him in this home through the Angel Board. Another visitor through the Angel Board was a Native American named Hamuck. Could it be a member of the Leni-Lenape tribe, who claimed the Mount Holly area as their home long before the European settlers made it theirs?

While Dave sorely misses his twin brother, he knows Fred's spirit lingers and he is watching over his family. His great-nephew has an imaginary friend whom he decided to name Fred, even though the child knew nothing of his great-uncle who had passed before his birth. When Dave asked his nephew what "Fred" looked like and presented an array of photos for his nephew to choose from, the young boy immediately pointed to a photo of Dave's late twin. The child had no idea he was choosing his late uncle.

Dave's historic home, guarded by gargoyles and a heavy gothic gate that Dave made himself, is steeped in Mount Holly history through several centuries and likely retains spirits from several periods of American history as well as art movements. Surely they would approve of the renovations done by this eccentric yet thoughtful artist, and are nodding their approval while enjoying his keen sense of humor. And while the presence of spirits is felt there by Dave, his sister and the neighbor next door, the frightening account of the Carr tragedy is, well, not quite as real as it is terrifying. Dave admits he conjured up the tale himself, as part of the Halloween fantasy he creates at his home every October. The plaque remains in front of his house, another artful strategy to strike terror in the hearts of those unsuspecting souls who read it while strolling by. It is part of the fun he has here and the mystique he creates about this elegantly eccentric home. He keeps his tradition of observing Halloween as a "high holy day of fun." You can almost hear the spirits chuckle.

Boo-geying Down Broad Street

Mount Holly's Broad Street is a beautiful, tree-shaded avenue in the historic district. In the first block is a group of Victorian homes that were part of a larger estate once owned by John Wardell Brown, a prominent Mount Holly lawyer. In the center of the Brown estate sits a pretty blue Victorian, decked out with white gingerbread. This home was built in 1890 and was then owned by Brown's nephew, a pastor at St. Andrew's Episcopal Church on High Street. Today it is the home of the McShulkis family. Mrs. McShulkis is a master gardener, and this is apparent as you admire the plantings and pottings separating this house from its neighbors on both sides. If you visit Mount Holly for Main Street Mount Holly's Hidden Garden Tour in June, you'll admire lush hostas of many varieties amongst aromatic lavender and bright ceramic pots and garden structures adorning the verandah. The pamphlet from the 2007 tour lists among the horticultural displays abundant heirloom plants, cold-hardy cactus and succulents, daffodils and prairie grasses that play like naughty children escaping the prudery of the

Victorian culture around the sides of the house. In the backyard, among the antique Monticello and English roses mingling with azaleas and garden structures, are residual plants of past owners, keeping a watchful eye on the newcomers to this historic garden.

This home wasn't always this lovely; Joe and Alicia McShulkis bought the house in February 2000 and worked for months before it was ready for their family to move in. John, their youngest son, went to school nearby at Sacred Heart on High Street. One day while Alicia was working downstairs on renovations, John came home from school and went upstairs while Alicia worked in the kitchen.

"Hey, Mom, who's that old lady upstairs in the front room?" John asked as he came down the steps.

"Not possible, John. I was here and nobody passed me to get upstairs. There is no way she could have gotten up there," Alicia tried to convince herself as well as her son, following John upstairs to see what he was talking about. Nobody was there when they entered the room. But John knows she was there, sitting at a window seat in the front room.

In May of that year, they completed renovations and moved in. As the kids got ready for bed one evening, Joe and Alicia watched TV. One by one the children came down the steps to say goodnight to their parents.

Several spirits keep watch over this pretty home.

"Goodnight," said John and went up to bed.

"Goodnight," said Joe and went up the stairs to bed.

"Goodnight," said Karine and she, too, went up to bed.

"Goodnight…" said ??? Both parents jolted and swung around. No child was there. They have only three children, but both had heard the voice of the fourth child.

Sometimes the feline members of the McShulkis family appear to be playing with a child, but nobody is there that the human family members can see. Who could these ghosts be?

"I'm not sure who it was but I know that we had one widowed homeowner who had two daughters from the turn of the century," says Alicia. She has also been told by neighbors that another woman lived there who had no children because her husband was killed in the war. She took in boarders.

Whoever the former mistress of the house was that checked in on the McShulkis family while they were renovating has not been back recently. Alicia thinks it is because the house is full of life again. "Personally, I think that whoever it was, was checking to see that the house was taken care of and there were kids here again," she said in an interview in October 2007.

But the cats still play with the unseen child.

**

Across the street, at 33 Broad Street, is a large white home believed to have been built in the late 1800s. The former owners would awaken in the morning to the sound of beautiful organ music. There was no organ in the home. These owners have since sold the house (whether because of musical ghosts is not known). The new owners have not reported any organ music, but have sensed a presence in this home since moving in early 2005.

"We have lots of occurrences of lights, especially basement and closet lights, being on in the morning when we are sure we turn them off at night," reports owner Michael Pierce. Pierce and his wife, Sharon Easterling, also report instances of closet doors opening and closing by themselves. Even their basset hound, Nietzsche, knows somebody is present other than his family. He will "sometimes be sleeping or lying awake peacefully and suddenly yelp and jump up as if scared or suddenly hit by something," says Pierce. Major remodeling has been in progress since Pierce and his wife moved in and bats living in the shutters of this house make Sharon and Michael feel that the spirits have had a hand in the decorating as well, Michael commented in October 2007.

**

Mystical music and prank playing spirits haunt this house.

Next door at 25 Broad Street is a large, impressive home that truly resembles a castle. It even has a porte-cochere, an architectural feature of many late eighteenth- and nineteenth-century mansions, built to allow residents and guests to leave their carriages and enter the home without falling victim to the effects of the elements. Everyone knows that every self-respecting castle has a ghost or two, and Mount Holly's version of a castle is not without its ghostly residents as well.

"Yes, I believe I have had a ghost here," says the "mistress" of the castle, Jean Messina.

Messina's home was built in 1894 by William Leconey Jr. of Moorestown for Benjamin Deacon. Originally, the porte-cochere had a pitched roof. From the 1920s through the 1970s, the home was owned by four generations of Coles. Bob and Jean Messina have a copy of the plans drawn up in August 1922 by Heacock & Hokanson of Philadelphia for then-homeowner Charles Coles. The plans called for altering the porte-cochere to flatten the roof. This gave it more of the castle look it has today.

The Messinas moved into this home in September of 1997, after the previous owners foreclosed. In the fall of 1998, their home was a designer

The haunted castle of Broad Street.

show house, a charity event for Zurbrugg/Lourdes. Prior to renovations on the kitchen and for the show house, Jean would hear the kitchen cabinets slam shut every morning at 4:30 a.m. During the show house, one of the designers who was decorating the third-floor family room saw a woman dressed in Victorian clothing on the third floor. She nodded her approval at the work that had been done and then vanished.

As you may imagine, a home as lovely as this is the perfect venue for holiday celebrations, and is often on the Mount Holly Holiday House Tour. Decked with Christmas greenery and decorations, friends and family gather for yuletide celebrations. Sometimes these celebrations are so warm and welcoming that they seem to entice some visitors from the other side to make an appearance. During holiday merriment in December 2006, one of the guests told Jean she felt a strong presence of a female ghost in the house. Then, when this guest left, an apparition appeared in her car and rode home with her. The ghost told the woman she had been falsely accused of murdering someone. The ghost pleaded with the woman to help her clear her name. She said the crime must be investigated and the record set straight.

Due to this incident, Jean stated in an interview in September 2007 that she is considering having her home investigated by professionals.

***

Also on the first block of Broad Street is another pretty Victorian home, a warm and friendly place that has been home to a young family since 2005 and a couple of ghosts for many years before that. When the young couple bought the house, they were aware it was haunted, the previous owners even claiming they had seen a ghost. It didn't really bother them. The husband has been haunted by ghosts in his past homes.

"My family has always been aware of ghosts, whether we choose to hunt them out or not. Ghosts always seem to find some way to entertain our family," he says as he recalls an incident in his childhood home when the former owner's sister and her boyfriend were seen in the basement of that home shortly after they had bought it. No, they weren't breaking in; they had been killed years before on their way home from Woodstock.

So, being used to living in a haunted house, the family immediately became friendly with one of their ghosts and decided to call him Bob. Bob plays tricks all the time. He turns the lights and ceiling fans on and off all during the day. Sometimes "we will come home from the shops late at night and the fan will be on full blast without any of the lights turned on or vice versa."

Bob likes to turn the lights off and on in the first-floor office, too. He also seems to get a little miffed when excluded from card games with the guys. One night, the owner had his buddies over to play cards. The owner told his friends about Bob and how he turns the lights off and on in the office, which was in full view of the room in which the guys were playing.

"Yeah, right."

"Sure, a ghost!"

They all laughed and made fun of any ghost in the house. Bob had the last laugh as he immediately began playing with the lights. Since nobody else was in the office and no one could control the lights from where they were, the card game immediately grew quiet. You could say Bob won that hand.

The other ghost is female, and the former owners described her as an older woman. She keeps to the third floor, or at least that is the only place in the house where she has been seen. This house is equipped with a doorbell inside the kitchen that only rings on the third floor.

"The only way to ring the bell is from the kitchen," explains the husband. "One early morning around 8:00 a.m., we were 'sleeping in' and heard the doorbell ring on the third floor. Obviously it was neither of us, as we were in bed at the time."

Was a gentleman caller from days gone by ringing up the old lady on the third floor? Coincidentally, this happened on Saturday the fourteenth, the day after the Haunted Holly Ghost Tour, held every Friday the thirteenth.

Maybe the ghost tour stirred up a sentimental old ghost who came calling for a lost love.

Steve, a friend of the family, is not too comfortable with his friends' housemates. "I will especially not go down in their basement. It's a dirt floor with an old coal chute. It's creepy. Who knows who died down there?"

THE HENRY FLENARD HOUSE

"The more enlightened our houses are, the more their walls ooze ghosts."
–*Italo Calvino,* The Literature Machine

Over at 138 Mill Street sits a historic home originally owned by Henry Flenard, born in 1820 and laid to rest in 1892 in the Mount Holly cemetery. Flenard had his home built in 1851 by the same builder who built the house next door. It is believed that the original structure consisted only of the two front rooms; the present-day kitchen and bathroom were likely added later. Bricks out back lead to nowhere now, but probably at one time led to the outdoor "loo."

"You will have a lot of happiness in this home," a man who grew up here told its current owner when she moved in in 1995. He didn't tell her she would also have a lot of company.

Five years after settling in, the current owner decided to remodel her dining room. Her daughter was getting married, and they would be hosting many prenuptial events and some out-of-town guests. That's when the spirits in her home began to make their presence known to her. The owner and her daughter began the task of painting the walls in the dining room. Evidently, the spirits in the home were displeased with the color she chose. For no reason, one of the dining room walls "oozed" with a liquid that was creamy in color and consistency. Thicker than water, yet not sticky, it just seeped out of a spot in the wall. There was nothing behind that wall, no plumbing, no leaks, no explanation.

"Spirits will do anything they can to get someone to notice them if that is what they are looking for," states South Jersey Ghost Research Director Dave Juliano. Dave has encountered this type of oozing manifestation on an investigation he did at a private home near Manyunk, outside of Philadelphia. That client went as far as having the wall ripped apart to see if there was an explanation for the oozing. "Contractors and home inspectors were unable to find any natural source and the house was actively haunted," says Dave of that similar experience. Juliano also comments in his book, *Ghost Research 101*, that liquids leaking from an unknown source could indicate that there is more going on than meets the eye.

The Henry Flenard house oozes with spirit activity.

During the dining room remodeling project, the owner and her daughter also heard voices speaking when nobody else was in the house besides them. On separate occasions, they each went into the bathroom, located near the dining room, closest to the wall that was oozing. While inside, each heard voices talking and thought someone had come into the house. It sounded like they were right outside the bathroom door. Upon exiting the bathroom, they found that nobody was there, or anywhere near there. Then they heard the door to the bedroom on the third floor close by itself, and there was no way it could do that.

The owner was distraught and did not know what to do about it. At the time, she lived there alone with her two daughters.

"I was so scared, I did not know what to do. I talked to people at work about it." A co-worker suggested she talk to the spirits. Being at a loss, she tried it. She asked them if they were not happy with the color of the paint. She painted it five or six different times. Still the walls oozed. Time was running out before the wedding and she did not have time to paint again, but she went to the local hardware store and bought new paint one last time. She presented it to the spirits and told them that as soon as she had time, she would repaint with this new color. They must have been satisfied. Finally, the oozing stopped, as mysteriously as it had started. But the owner would lie in bed at night and still hear somebody walking around the house.

One day, a woman came to Mount Holly for her sixtieth high school class reunion. She was born in the Henry Flenard house in 1924. She stopped by her childhood home and knocked on the door. The owner's daughter was home at the time, and let her see her old home. The older woman asked the daughter if her mother was the one who removed the wallpaper in the dining room. The daughter said that someone else must have done it, as it was not on the walls when they bought the house. "My parents loved that wallpaper," the older woman said.

Though the oozing has stopped, the owner and her boyfriend still frequently hear activity at night and they feel a presence in the house, years after the remodeling episode. "Sometimes we hear somebody down in the kitchen late at night, doing dishes. When this happens, you just lay there petrified."

Over the years, the owner has made peace with the spirits, who still remain. In a way, she sometimes feels now like they are looking out for her well-being, as she recalls the case of a personal incident that could have had a big impact on her life. She and her boyfriend were having a difficult time and decided the best thing to do would be to separate. She felt they had made the right decision and she was prepared to begin a new, single life again. Then, one night when he was away for business, she went searching for her prior year's tax records, which she stored in the third-floor bedroom. She reached for the light switch, but the light would not go on. She knew the bulb was new. With no light at the bottom of the stairs, she crawled up the stairs in darkness and felt her way across the bedroom to a small table lamp on the other side of the room. When she turned on the light, she saw her boyfriend's belongings packed in boxes. Suddenly it hit her, and the realization of his leaving knotted her stomach. At that moment she knew it was the wrong decision. When he returned, she talked to him about it and they decided to try to stay together and work their issues out. Then she asked him about the bulb. When she walked back to it that night to examine it, it had been unscrewed. She asked him why he did that. He said he hadn't touched it. The "light bulb" in her head at that moment flashed on, as she knew the spirits were watching and trying to get her to reconsider. If she hadn't seen those packed boxes, he would have just left without her reconsidering her decision and talking to him about reconciliation. And she would never have seen those packed boxes back in that far alcove of the third-floor bedroom if she had not had to crawl across the room in the darkness to turn on that table lamp over on that far side of the room.

Peace has been made with the spirits at 138 Mill Street. It is a happy home, with family and ghosts abiding in harmony. The dining room has yet to be repainted, but the paint cans hold the promise and the spirits are so far being patient.

Ghosts and Human Relationships

The owner of the Henry Flenard house is not alone in having a ghost intervene in her personal relationship. Many others have had such paranormal meddling in their affairs and one is Mount Holly resident Kyle Miller. Before Kyle lived in a couple haunted houses in Mount Holly, she grew up on a farm in nearby Vincentown. When she was fourteen years old, she began dating an older boy for a while. One night while on the phone with her boyfriend, a woman appeared in a lace dress. This woman looked at her very sternly and gave her a look of fierce disapproval. Then she disappeared into thin air. Kyle threw the phone down and ran down the hall looking for the woman, but she could not find her. The admonition of the apparition so unnerved Kyle that she did end the relationship with the boy.

A few years later, Kyle began dating another young man. He took her home after the second date and kissed her goodnight at the door of the old farmhouse. Then he walked back to his car, which was parked in the long driveway that led to the farmhouse. Kyle stayed at the door to wave goodbye and watch him drive off. He started up his car and began to drive away. Suddenly, he stopped for a moment. Then he gunned the engine, his wheels spun, gravel flew in all directions and he sped out of the driveway.

Kyle waited until he could get home and then gave him a call, concerned over what could have caused his erratic driving. Shaking, he told her that he thought he had seen a ghost. He described a woman in a lace dress, standing in the driveway near his car.

"What did she do?" Kyle asked, anxiously awaiting his reply and remembering the disparaging gestures of this woman several years ago, which caused Kyle to end that relationship.

"She was just nodding her approval; I don't know about what, but it was freaky," he replied, still shaking from the experience. A few years later, they were married.

Kyle had described the apparition she saw years before, and that her husband had apparently seen more recently, to older neighbors and family members. She asked them if they had any idea who it may be. She was told of a young woman who had lived in a farmhouse that used to be adjacent to the one Kyle grew up in. That farmhouse had caught on fire and the young woman died of smoke inhalation. She was only in her thirties, but she was in an unhappy marriage. Her husband was abusive to her. Kyle feels she must have been watching over her home for a while and passing judgment on the men that called. She remembered that even some of her father's male company would often not stay long; they felt uncomfortable and would make excuses to leave early.

Kyle and her husband moved to Mount Holly in 1994. Before purchasing their current Madison Avenue home, they lived at 148 Greenwood Avenue. When they first moved in, they were often awakened between four and five o'clock in the morning by the sound of footsteps in the attic above their bed. It sounded like a small child in hard-soled shoes running back and forth. Since they had no children, there was no explanation for this. Kyle even went up to the attic one day and spread powder on the floor, to see if by any chance a child was somehow getting into their attic. Again they heard the footsteps, but when she went to the attic, there were no footprints on the powdered floor. It was a calm night, and there was no wind or anything that could be causing this sound. They didn't know what it could be, but were tired of being awakened by this misbehaving youngster, if that's what it was. The next night it happened, Kyle and her husband went up to the attic and asked "him" to please be quiet because "he" was waking them up. Maybe the child didn't realize he was misbehaving; they never heard the sound again.

"It's sad; it sounded like a happy child playing," says Kyle. "It's a shame this spirit died so young."

Next door, at 146 Greenwood Avenue, the neighbors encountered an old woman in the basement. She just appeared to them, but then vanished. The wife was afraid to go into the basement to do laundry because of the ghost, although she caused them no harm.

Kyle's mother-in-law lived at 152 Greenwood Avenue. After she died, Kyle's sister-in-law and aunt rearranged all the dishes in the china cabinet. The mother-in-law would not have liked the way they displayed her china, but they didn't think much about it—until they left the room, came back ten minutes later and saw that all the china was back the way the mother-in-law had left it.

Today, this neighborhood on the western side of town is merely a ghost itself. All the homes on Greenwood Avenue and several other streets in that area have been demolished to make way for the expansion of the Mount Holly campus of Virtua Hospital.

Kyle and her husband moved to nearby Madison Avenue. Their home is a brick ranch, circa 1950. Kyle believes another structure was probably on the property years ago. There is sunken ground on the edge of the property between her home and the colonial that stands next door. She thinks that maybe it was a root cellar in days gone by.

On three separate occasions, Kyle has seen a soldier standing at the bottom of her cellar steps, looking in anticipation up the stairs as if he is waiting for someone, yet he looks right through Kyle. He is in uniform, and Kyle thinks it is a Civil War uniform. A handsome young man, he has dark, mutton chop sideburns.

Blowin' in the Wind

The Lost Village of Timbuctoo

"Yes, 'n how many ears must one man have before he can hear people cry? Yes, 'n how many deaths will it take till he knows that too many people have died?"
—Bob Dylan

Less than a century after being a battleground for the American Revolution, Mount Holly found itself again smack in the center of controversy during the War Between the States. Slave ownership and abolition, fierce issues of the Civil War, were hotly condemned in orations by Quaker leaders such as Mount Holly's John Woolman. Quakers were plentiful in Mount Holly and surrounding areas, and it is probably due to the populous Quaker settlement here that the Delaware Valley has been called by some "The Cradle of Emancipation." Mount Holly was a stop on one route of the Underground Railroad. Beck writes in *The Jersey Midlands* that one official of that historic, clandestine system reportedly said of the Underground Railroad, "I think the machine was better oiled among the Friends and so worked more smoothly."

Some historians claim that the success and size of the Underground Railroad have been greatly exaggerated, and are busy debunking myths concerning the routes and stops along this covert passage to freedom. "Slaves who ran away and came north constituted a very small percentage of the overall number of slaves who ran away. Most runaways stayed in the South and did not come north. That is why we can discount a lot of the claims that have been made about the Underground Railroad—because we have almost more claimed sites than we have slaves," states New Jersey historian Giles Wright. Wright contends that during the approximately thirty-one years of the nineteenth century that the Underground Railroad operated, thirty to fifty thousand slaves are estimated to have passed through it, at a time when there were a total of about four million slaves throughout the United States. This means that barely 1 percent of all slaves escaped to the North, reported Hoag Levins in the *Historic Camden County News*.

The Hazelhurst-Ashurst Mansion in Mount Holly is reported to have been one of the stops along the Underground Railroad, according to Rizzo, and a little community along the Rancocas Creek in Westampton, on the edge of Mount Holly, was a refuge for free black citizens and runaway slaves. Wright himself has validated the history of Timbuctoo, or "Bucktu" as this enclave came to be known, and has substantiated the armed showdown between runaway slaves and slave catchers that took place in Timbuctoo in the 1860s, which became known as the Battle of Pine Swamp.

Timbuctoo seems to have been established around 1820 but, it may have been founded as early as the late eighteenth century with the support of local Quakers like John Woolman and Samuel Aaron. It took its name from a West African city and was possibly the only all-black settlement in the nation carrying the name of an African community, although there is uncertainty as to how it came to be called Timbuctoo. Many of its inhabitants were skilled in various trades and owned their own property. At its peak of prosperity in the mid- to late nineteenth century (it appears on an 1849 map of Burlington County), it had more than 125 residents, a school and an AME Zion church. The Burlington County History and Tourism website reports that it also served as a site for religious revivals, attracting large crowds to Bucktu.

Many "riders" on the Underground Railroad did not attain the freedom they sought, and are buried in the woods near Timbuctoo. Perinchief writes in *History of Cemeteries in Burlington County*, "They died en route and their place of burial had to be concealed from the relentless searchers of runaways. Negro residents who are descendants of some of these former slaves remember tales told by their grandparents. Those who did not make freedom were interred in the woods near Rancocas."

In 1860, a slave catcher came to Timbuctoo with several Mount Holly residents to capture a fugitive slave, Percy Simmons. In the ensuing Battle of Pine Swamp, residents of Timbuctoo took up arms to prevent the capture of Simmons. Several people were injured in the skirmish, but Simmons was not captured. "This incident," says Giles Wright, "underscores why these all-black settlements are of particular importance as havens that provided runaway slaves with a great deal of safety."

This was not the only attempt to capture Simmons, who died in 1862 in Timbuctoo, as reported by the *New Jersey Mirror*, a local paper of the time. Simmons had been ill since the last attempt to capture him, when he lay freezing at night on the ground, hiding from his ensuing captors. Finally, the *New Jersey Mirror* recounted, he was "beyond the reach of his Southern master."

A site steeped with such history, agony and emotion is bound to have a ghost or two. In February 1929, the *New York Times* reported an incident of three ghosts, two white and one black, appearing in Timbuctoo. At that time, the little hamlet was home to about one hundred residents. The spirits appeared at the home of Walter Treichler, a retired chemist. Treichler had been awakened by tapping, footsteps and moaning after midnight. A posse of investigators came to his home to explore the possibility of ghosts haunting his residence. A spiritualist medium, detectives and some armed police officers participated. They found nothing that night, but Burlington County Chief of Detectives Ellis Parker, a celebrated law enforcement official who was better known for his work in the Charles Lindbergh kidnapping case, conceded that romance and mystery have always surrounded the Treichler house.

At one time, it was the site of the Jug Tavern, run by Cy Jenkins and his wife, known by the clientele as Aunt Harriet. Cy died at age ninety and his wife continued operating the tavern; that is, until she disappeared. It was believed she was robbed and murdered. Every ten years after her death, there were reports of strange happenings and reports of ghost sightings. The *New York Times* article reported there were always ghosts in Timbuctoo.

Some old-timers spoke of the "Bucktu" ghosts and some also remembered a "witch house" there. Beck writes, "There was the Witch House," recalled a Mrs. Warwick who lived in nearby Rancocas, recalling spooky happenings in Timbuctoo when she was a child. "There was a strange old woman who lived there when we were girls. We used to hurry by, wondering."

Today the community is a ghost town itself. Timbuctoo, a small village playing a big part in American history, once alive with song and revival while at the same time facing turmoil and uncertainty, is today marked by little more than a cemetery on Church Street containing the graves of black Civil War veterans.

There are no records of burials in this small cemetery and very few tombstones. At one time, a church stood in the forefront of the graveyard, but it was torn down in the 1940s. Old residents of the area say that the grounds used to be much larger and the slave graves are back in the woods. The earliest stone is that of Eliza Parker, who died in 1847. Perinchief reports that she was fourteen years old.

Could this little Parker girl be one who has haunted this village, taken at such an early age? Or Percy Simmons, who spent so many years fighting his master's henchmen, sent to return him to slavery? Or other runaway slaves

Not much remains of the old Timbuctoo village. There's a small graveyard of black Civil War veterans…oh, and a few ghosts.

who suffered and died during their quest for freedom in the North, and are buried in the woods behind Bucktu? These souls, tortured on earth, some finding refuge in this little village, may have returned to the one place they found safety, freedom and acceptance.

Terror on the Mount

"I know a mount, the gracious Sun perceives;
First when he visits, last, too, when he leaves the world."
–Robert Browning

B urlington County is the largest New Jersey county in area, stretching from the Pinelands to the industrial bedroom communities of Philadelphia. Mount Holly is the county seat of Burlington County, and is located toward its northern end. With towns having names like Mount Holly and Mount Laurel, you would maybe think of our area as quite elevated. But most of the land in Burlington County is considerably flat. Whenever an area has any elevation at all it seems it gets tagged a "mount." The highest point in elevation is Arney's Mount, in nearby Springfield Township, which has the distinction of being the highest point of elevation between New Brunswick, New Jersey (the county seat of Middlesex County), and Washington, D.C. It rises 229.4 feet above sea level. A Springfield Township historian claims that this "mount" was formed about twenty-one million years ago and that it was once under the ocean, as reported in the *Courier Post*.

Arney's Mount was originally called Shreve's Mount, named for Caleb Shreve, whose family was one of the first to settle in this area. At the crossroads near the foot of this "mount" sits the Arney's Mount Friends Meeting House, a building made from locally quarried sandstone. The Arney's Mount Friends were formed in 1743, after Friends from the upper part of the Mount Holly Meeting requested from the Burlington Monthly Meeting the liberty to hold meetings "at the meeting house at Caleb Shreve's mount." The land was conveyed to the Quakers for one shilling "for a meeting house thereon and a place to bury their dead," reports Perinchief.

This meetinghouse and the surrounding area are rife with ghost stories and were investigated by South Jersey Ghost Research on a partly cloudy evening in September of 2001. According to their website, the researchers did find spirit activity there, as well as in the surrounding burial ground, which predates the building.

Mount Holly is proud to claim its own mesa, for which it gets its name. About seven miles from Arney's Mount, it rises above the plains of relatively flat South Jersey, and today is simply known around town as "the Mount." This parcel of real estate was originally called Cripps's Mount, after John Cripps, who arrived in America aboard the *Kent*, and who built the first house in Mount Holly. Tradition has it that he climbed the elevation searching for a plot for his home and was so pleased with the view and the holly on the hill that he purchased the property, Perinchief writes. Nobody seems to know exactly where his abode was, but it is speculated that it was north of "the Mount." Cripps is also credited with giving Mount Holly its name, in dedication to this mount, which was crowned with beautiful holly trees, Shinn reports in his *History of Mount Holly*. Mount Holly's namesake plateau rises 185 feet above sea level. There are two National Geodetic markers on the top of the mount, probably placed there in 1840, during the Coast and Geodetic Survey.

Across town is another small rising, once known as Top-e-toy. Around Christmas time in 1776, Colonel Samuel Griffin gathered a small band of Patriots around Top-e-toy and the nearby ironworks on the south side of the

The Mount overlooks the town of Mount Holly, and is how it got its name. *Photo courtesy of Mount Holly Historical Society.*

Rancocas Creek. To catch the attention of the Redcoats and divert them from Trenton, Griffin then sent about six hundred troops to attack the Scots at Petticoate Bridge in what is now Springfield Township. This enraged Colonel Von Donop, who took all his Hessian troops and marched them to Mount Holly. With the Hessians and their cannons set up on the Mount, and the colonial forces at Top-e-toy, the Battle of Mount Holly was waged, probably where the mansions of High Street stand today. The big guns of the Hessians overpowered the Americans and their smaller cannons, and Von Donop pushed the Americans back to their trenches. During the night, the Americans retreated to Moorestown, and Von Donop ransacked Mount Holly and celebrated his victory. His stay in Mount Holly, of course, led to Washington claiming victory in Trenton.

Long since the days of Joseph Cripp and the battles of the American Revolution, the Mount has witnessed many changes over the years and has captured the mystic and legend of many. It rises above the Mount Holly cemetery, which may give rise to some of the supernatural stories surrounding the Mount. A reservoir was dug there, and today is replaced by a water tower.

In an interview in November 2007, longtime Mount Holly resident Larry Tigar remembered,

> *In 1925 or 1926 the army built an observation tower on top of the mount. By all accounts you could see the Delaware River at Burlington and at night you could clearly see the lights of Philadelphia. It was only there about six months and was torn down mainly because local kids insisted on climbing it. The Mount has been used by kids and adults alike for sleighing in winter. One of the Elbertson boys broke his leg when he wrapped it around a tree when he failed to make a curve. I used to play on the Mount occasionally when I was young but not on a regular basis.*

Religious ceremonies were held on the Mount over the years. "Easter sunrise services were held for many years on the Mount. My dad remembers hearing the singing while he was on the horse wagon delivering milk," says Larry.

Although I know of no professional ghost hunters who have investigated the Mount, a place as eerie as this has garnered local interest and is fodder for ghost stories. Stories abound of devil worship ceremonies up there. Some local children also believe that a witch is buried in the well on the Mount. If you dare to walk up there today, you will find an old altar with the words "Holy, Holy, Holy" engraved in the stone. The altar was used for the religious ceremonies of bygone days, but has obviously been the victim of vandals or some other evildoers, as it is badly worn, battered and beaten. The well is covered by a small house-like structure.

According to Moran and Sceurman's *Weird NJ*, legend has it that the witch was thrown into the well, still alive. She screamed and banged on the walls of the well, bloodying her hands, begging to be saved. She died in the well and some say you could hear her screams and the sounds of her knuckles banging against the wall of the well. So they built a shed over the well so you couldn't hear her. The children say if you go up there at night and knock on the walls of the shed, she will knock back.

Former High Street Grill waiter Brian Strumfels will attest to the spookiness of the Mount. "About four or five years ago, I went up there myself in the winter. I saw the shack where the witch was supposedly thrown in, and I saw hoof prints on the ground. There is a creepy, spooky atmosphere up there."

One grim tale of the Mount claims that a celebrity of sorts may have met his demise there. The Jersey Devil, supposedly born almost three hundred years ago to a woman in Leeds Point, about fifty miles away from Mount Holly, was the thirteenth child of Mrs. Leeds, a very unwelcome thirteenth child.

"Let this one be a devil!" she cried when she found out she was pregnant. Exhausted from her poverty-stricken life of perpetual childbirth, Mrs. Leeds cursed the child as she was giving birth, as well as her drunkard husband. While the child was born normal, he momentarily morphed into a monster! Mrs. Leeds watched in horror as her prenatal wish came true. She saw her thirteenth child grow the wings of a huge bat, the body of a red horse, horns on its head, talons on its fingers and the tail of a serpent. The monster's first act was to savagely kill his own mother before moving on to destroy the rest of his family. He then flew out of his natal home, some say through the chimney, and began to live his life terrorizing those unlucky souls who found themselves alone at night in the Jersey Pinelands. The Pinelands at night are spooky enough, even without a creature like the Jersey Devil roaming about, but his destruction of land and livestock has made many feel unsafe to ride down some of the lonely back roads alone at night.

The Jersey Devil has been reported to find occasion to sometimes leave the Pinelands. Maybe he gets bored with country life sometimes and seeks the city lights. He has been reported to be seen as far away as Burlington, Camden and Haddon Heights, and even across the river in Bristol and Philadelphia. It seems the Jersey Devil is sighted in New Jersey as often as Elvis in Vegas.

One legend has it that the Jersey Devil is chained up and sealed inside the altar on the Mount. Some say that if you put your ear to it, you can hear his

Can this altar cap a shaft that goes to hell, and holds the Jersey Devil captive?

chains clanging against the stone. They say the altar caps a shaft that goes all the way to hell. The Mount Holly cemetery, lying at the foot of the Mount, supposedly holds the grave of the woman who summoned the Jersey Devil to his demise on the Mount, Moran and Sceurman claim.

You would think the Jersey Devil would be at the top of everyone's most despised list for his evil deeds and frightening demeanor. Yet, the Jersey Devil is probably the best-loved, or at least most well-known, of all New Jersey supernatural folklore, even having a professional hockey team named after him. If his life has ended, it would be exciting to think he rests in peace in Mount Holly. But how dispiriting to think of him as gone from rural South Jersey. Call me a hopeless romantic, I guess; I'd rather think of the Jersey Devil as still alive and well, kicking up his horse-hooved heels and terrorizing the nearby New Jersey Pinelands.

Mount Holly Cemeteries

"We approach all cemeteries we encounter with great respect for the property and for the deceased. Cemeteries are full of our history and they need to be preserved and treated with reverence."
—*South Jersey Ghost Research website*

There are about a half-dozen cemeteries in Mount Holly. While cemetery property should be treated with respect, in reverence for those passed on, let's admit it—they can be creepy, scary places. The vultures perching on the tombstones every morning and evening at the Sacred Heart Cemetery certainly contribute to making that perception a reality. It can be an eerie sight. "They were rocking the trees as I entered the cemetery last week…it looked as if the trees were fully leafed out, but they were rustling and moving. Then, I realized it wasn't leaves in the trees—it was an amazing hoard of the turkey vultures…right at dusk," recalled Mount Holly resident Jean Messina about the ominous birds inhabiting the cemetery.

But why should we be scared of cemeteries? It seems from what we have learned from the residents and business owners in Mount Holly that the ghosts are haunting the buildings, the places where they spent their lives, not their final resting places. Do we really need to be afraid of cemeteries?

Let's ask that question of Dave Juliano, director of South Jersey Ghost Research (SJGR). SJGR has investigated the Sacred Heart Cemetery, where the first person buried was Thomas Foy, in 1857. Foy was a devout Catholic who lived in the Bass house at 25 Church Street, one of the oldest streets in Mount Holly. Winzinger and Smith claim that Foy was a generous contributor to Mount Holly's Church of the Sacred Heart.

Professional ghost hunters have seen spirits walking around this cemetery.

"There have been spirits of a couple in their twenties walking around together and I did witness them, along with a few others when I was there," says Juliano of one of his investigations at the burial ground of Thomas Foy. "We have also investigated a house near the cemetery that had the spirit of a young boy that was coming into their home and manifesting for short periods of time, then he would go back to the cemetery."

Over on Pine Street is Saint Andrew's Cemetery. It stands near where the colonial army was stationed during the Battle of Iron Works Hill. A wooden church, chartered by King George III in 1765, and the original Episcopal Church in Mount Holly stood on the site at one time. Today, Perinchief notes that this cemetery area also includes Trinity Episcopal and the Baptist Cemeteries. Steven Carty lives on Herald Street, which is right off Pine Street, bordering the cemetery. He claims that on several nights he has heard the lonesome sound of a solo bagpiper playing "Scotland the Brave." Others have also reported hearing bagpipe music coming from St. Andrew's Cemetery.

One early spring evening in the early 1970s, a group of young boys ran around the tombstones, playing hide and seek. The days were just beginning to get longer and warmer and they stayed out past dusk. Though told to be

Who wants to play at St. Andrew's Cemetery?

home "before the streetlights came on," they lost track of time, enjoying the first break of vernal warmth. Absorbed in their game and intoxicated with spring fever, it took a while before they noticed that someone had joined them who hadn't been there from the beginning. In the twilight hours it was hard to make him out at first, but as a couple of the boys approached him, they saw he was slightly disfigured, and then…he just faded into the twilight air. Realizing they had just witnessed a partial apparition, they screamed and cried to the rest of their friends to run. Almost tripping over each other as they ran out of the driveway and onto Pine Street, shrieking in horror, they knew it was the last time they would be playing that game in a cemetery.

Perinchief writes that April 20, 1841, is the day the first grave was dug at the Mount Holly cemetery on Ridgeway Street. This sprawling graveyard lies at the base of the Mount, which looks over all of Mount Holly and is the object of many scary stories passed among youngsters in town. According to Moran and Sceurman in *Weird NJ*, a young woman's gravestone in the Mount Holly cemetery contains the epitaph, "Thus is the fate of all who turn from God." Legend has it that she summoned the Jersey Devil to Mount Holly. He killed her but then he was captured, chained and buried under the altar up on the Mount.

Nestled at the foot of the Mount, this graveyard probably has many stories to tell.

"A change in point of view is probably the best way to describe death," wrote Tom Butler in "What We Know about Life after Death." While you could wonder how those resting in peace in Mount Holly's cemeteries view what goes on around them, it's probably those not resting so peacefully we need to be concerned about.

The Old Burlington
County Courthouse

"Mere access to the courthouse doors does not by itself assure a proper functioning of the adversary process."
—Thurgood Marshall

This beautiful old building that sits on High Street, in sharp contrast to the nearby gray macabre-looking Burlington County Prison Museum, was built amid much controversy and regional rivalry near the end of the eighteenth century. Burlington County had a courthouse in Burlington city, which had been the county seat since 1693. When that building fell into disrepair, an election was held to determine where the new courthouse should be built, and the location selected would be named the county seat. The county had developed considerably since Burlington city was anointed with county administration authority one hundred years prior, so it was thought by some that the hub should be moved toward the center of the county. The hotly contested referendum, held in February of 1795, pitted Burlington, Mount Holly and Black Horse (now known as Columbus) against each other as candidates. When Mount Holly was selected as the site for the courthouse and therefore the new county seat, the residents of Burlington were up in arms about the audacity of the "Mount Hollians" for "robbing them of the pride, ornament and source of influence of their native city," writes Shinn. The residents of Burlington went so far as to accuse that "charcoal burners from the pines voted with blackened faces and then washed them in the creek and voted again under another name," Perinchief reports in *History of Cemeteries in Burlington County*. It began a rivalry between the two towns that endured until all residents alive at that time were long deceased.

Despite the displeasure of Burlington city, a lot was purchased on High Street and upon it was built one of the finest examples of colonial architecture in the nation, designed by Samuel Lewis, architect for Congress Hall in Philadelphia. Mr. Lewis was married to Rachel Dobbins of Mount Holly. Shinn notes that the contractor was Michael Rush, who also built the woodwork of the Friends Meeting House.

Upon completion of the elegant chambers, the New Jersey Coat of Arms was hung over the door, and a bell cast in England in 1755 that once hung in the old Burlington courthouse was obtained to ring for court sessions. Tradition says the bell also once rang when news of the signing of the Declaration of Independence reached Burlington. The new courthouse in Mount Holly held its first session in November of 1796, underwent major renovations in the early 1990s and is still used by the New Jersey Judiciary as a courtroom today for chancery and civil division cases. The DAR's *Historic Mount Holly, New Jersey*, reports that the courthouse, the two buildings flanking it (built as the surrogate's office and the collector's office in 1807)

The beautiful Burlington County Courthouse, built amidst much local rivalry, condemned many souls to its basement jail.

and the adjacent Burlington County Prison (now the museum) is the largest group of county buildings in continuous use since colonial times.

The basement of this old building originally contained about forty prison cells. One notable guest held in these cold stone cells in 1796 was Supreme Court Justice James Wilson, a signer of the Declaration of Independence. Wilson fell into debt over several bad land deals and was held in prison here on debtors' charges. His son paid his debt and freed him from jail, and he died two years later in North Carolina. However, several other prisoners did meet the grim reaper in the basement of this historic court building, whose jail continued to hold prisoners in the basement until the construction of the adjacent Burlington County Prison in 1811.

In January of 1893, the Burlington County Courthouse was mobbed as the town crammed its halls to witness a real local cause célèbre: the murder trial of Wesley Warner. When found guilty, Warner spent the next several months, the last of his life, next door at the Burlington County Prison, awaiting his execution as sentenced by Judge Garrison.

The old courthouse is beautifully restored and still in use today by judiciary staff...and a few spirits.

"This building has a life of its own," claims one courthouse source, who prefers to remain anonymous. "People don't want to be here alone." The unexplainable sounds and happenings are a constant discussion topic among staff and maintenance workers. Strange sounds, slamming doors and creaking are constant. A faint tapping, with no attributable source, is often heard.

Court officials are considering having the building inspected by professional ghost researchers. According to Dave Juliano of South Jersey Ghost Research, his investigators would love to have a shot at checking out this interesting, historic old building. Here you have a beautifully constructed building, yet built among animosity and rivalry between towns; courtroom activity that hears and passes judgment on the trials and tribulations of many souls, from thieves and murderers to Supreme Court justices; and cells that imprisoned many unfortunate souls, even claiming some. So much emotion and personal tragedy lead to the possibility for souls to get lost and confused, to linger at the site that held them captive or took away their happiness.

So, if court administrators are trying to prove to staff that ghosts are not present, well, they should be aware they may get the opposite result. Just ask the freeholders in office in 1999, who tried that at the neighboring Burlington County Prison Museum. The fears of workers there were confirmed by the ghost researchers. What will the court managers tell the staff then? Maybe not much they don't already know.

The Mount Holly
Witch Trial

"Heed ye flower, bush and tree, by the Lady blessed be. Where the rippling waters flow,
cast a stone and truth ye'll know."
–from the Wiccan Rede

Mount Holly has for many years celebrated the fall season and Halloween with an annual event that attracts hundreds of revelers from throughout the area. Always held the second weekend in October and originally called the Witches' Ball, in 2007 the name and format changed, creating two distinctly different festivals on the same evening. One is called Sleepy Holly, complete with a visit from the Headless Horseman, and another starting later in the evening, the Cirque de la Lune, showcases aerialists, ghost researchers, fire-eaters and other fascinating characters. These October events in Mount Holly welcome the fall season and the Halloween holiday, a favorite holiday for many, and pagan in origin. Halloween, originally All Hallow's Eve, is the night before the Wiccan holiday of Samhain. A Celtic word that means "summer's end," Samhain is a Wiccan day of reverence for their honored dead.

While the caricature of the witch, with her green scaly skin and long bumpy nose, cavorting about on a broom and accompanied by a black cat, is popular at Halloween festivals and parties, the true story of witches is sometimes a sad one. A witch was at one time respected as a wise woman and a healer, but as Christianity grew in popularity in Europe, the witch became maligned as someone anxious to cast a pox upon you. Their doom began in 1487, when two priests wrote *Malleus Maleficarum*, a witch hunting manual. The website Sacredtexts.com writes that this marked the beginning of the genocide of

Even the Headless Horseman visits Mount Holly.

thousands of people, primarily women, who were hunted down, tortured and murdered as a result of the procedures described in this book, sometimes for no reason other than a strange birthmark, living alone, mental illness, cultivation of medicinal herbs, or simply because they were falsely accused (often for financial gain by the accuser)... The Malleus *was used as a judicial case-book for the detection and persecution of witches, specifying rules of evidence and the canonical procedures by which suspected witches were tortured and put to death. The* Malleus *serves as a horrible warning about what happens when intolerence* [sic] *takes over a society.*

Ironically Wicca, the religion of many witches, is actually an earth-based religion celebrating the seasons, the stewardship of the environment and respect and reverence for all creatures, so casting evil upon others would not be on a witch's to-do list.

Misunderstanding the witches' true peaceful ideology, this intolerance of them and their pagan ways intensified and crossed the Atlantic with the Puritans, made famous with the Salem witch trials. Then, in October

1730 an article appeared in the *Pennsylvania Gazette*, a publication owned by Benjamin Franklin. Some credit Ben himself with penning this story of a witchcraft trial held in Mount Holly. In the article, a man and a woman were accused of singing psalms, causing their neighbors to dance like sheep and causing hogs to speak, all "to the great terror and amazement of the King's good and peaceable subjects in this province."

It was decided by the general populace that these two "witches" must be tried via tests, and eager to prove their innocence, the two agreed, as long as two of their accusers would be put to the same test. The first test was their individual weights against a Bible. The idea was that if they were heavier than the Bibles, they could not be witches. When all four were weighed and proven to be heavier than the "Holy Writ," the crowd demanded another test. It was decided all four would be thrown into a pond and if they floated, they would be revealed as witches. The mob marched them to the millpond, the four were stripped, "saving only to the women their shifts," and they were thrown into the pond from a barge, bound hand and foot. All

Mount Holly's October celebrations bring out a diverse party crowd.

four floated to the top, yet the accused women were thought to have used witchcraft to make themselves float or that possibly their shifts caused them to float. Since that cast doubt on the validity of the test, it was decided to have the trial again in warmer weather and all would be naked.

It is not known whether the retrial ever occurred, or if the story is even true. While it provided gripping reading for Philadelphians and was reprinted in a British publication, the *Gentleman's Gazette*, some historians of Franklin's work believe it was just a satirical piece of journalism. It never appeared locally in any publication other than Franklin's own, and since witch trials had waned in frequency by that time (the Salem witch trials took place forty years earlier) it would have been more widely publicized had it been true. Franklin most likely wrote it as a parody of Puritan beliefs at the time, revealing that "by 1730 it had become acceptable for the educated class in America to ridicule beliefs such as witchcraft, even though the majority of the population still clung to those beliefs," according to the Museum of Hoaxes website.

Blessed be that Mount Holly is today focused on more celebratory functions.

The Mill Street Tavern

"May your glass be ever full, May the roof over your head be always strong, And may you be in heaven half an hour before the devil knows you're dead."
—Irish drinking toast

Located at the convergence of Mill and Pine Streets, the Mill Street Tavern is the oldest standing building in Mount Holly. A tavern and a hotel since it was first opened in 1723, it was built with walls fourteen inches thick. While believed to be haunted itself, it has also contributed to the haunting of at least one other important building in Mount Holly. Vanscivers, as the tavern was called in 1892, was the last public building visited by Wesley Warner before he lay in wait to murder his mistress, who was returning to her home on Pine Street after visiting the opera with friends. Mr. Warner's spirit is one of those believed to haunt the Burlington County Prison Museum, where he lived his final days before being hanged there on September 6, 1894.

The Mill Street Tavern was built about forty years after the first settlers arrived in Mount Holly. There appeared to be a need for a place for rest and libation, so the Three Tuns Tavern was built near the mill in Mount Holly, at that time called Bridgetown because of all the bridges over the various feeders to the Rancocas Creek. It most likely got its original name from the casks, or "tuns," kept in arched vaults in the cellar. Samuel Brian was the first owner and innkeeper, and few changes have been made to the building since his time. It is the oldest inn in Mount Holly and was grabbed as quarters by the Hessian soldiers during their occupation here in 1776, the DAR reports. Winzinger and Smith note that handbills for runaway slaves were posted here, and the establishment has also had many names and nicknames through the years, including the Bucket of Blood and Vanscivers.

There may be more patrons bellying up to the bar at the Mill Street Tavern than meets the eye.

It is claimed that John Woolman, the prominent Mount Holly Quaker, went there, not to imbibe but rather to try to squash a magic show being staged there. Although legerdemain was legal in Mount Holly in 1763, Woolman was troubled by it and when handbills heralded the arrival of sleight of hand performers for a show at the tavern, Woolman sat at the door quoting scripture and trying to steer patrons away. He left before the show began, feeling he had done what he could to dissuade patrons from attending, write Milbourne and Milbourne in *The Illustrated History of Magic*.

Today, Pavo Leno manages the bar at this historic tavern, and while he and some of his bartenders don't like to discuss the ghosts haunting his establishment, he does not deny they exist. He proudly tells how his tavern was always a bar and a hotel and that it was also a stagecoach stop. There were once separate entrances for men and women. Then, after much coaxing, he begins to tell about the noises and banging coming from downstairs. He will sometimes leave the bar and go down to investigate; there is never any cause for the sound. His customers have felt someone touch them upon their shoulders. They turn around on their bar stools, expecting to welcome a drinking buddy to sit down and share a brew, only to find there is nobody there. Sometimes the door slams as if somebody just came in. Again, no one is there.

Once, a rather heavy woman, about four hundred pounds, was sitting at the bar. "She thought somebody 'goosed' her," chuckles Leno, as he remembers her rising about four feet off her bar stool. Again, there was no visible cause for the grab she felt to her derriére.

"If only the walls could talk," says Leno.

Home Fine Art

"Illusions are art, for the feeling person, and it is by art that you live, if you do."
–Elizabeth Bowen

Mount Holly artists Jim and Lynn Lemyre live in a house built by Samuel White, a master carpenter, in 1875. Upon moving into the home in December of 2000, friends offered, as a housewarming gift, to do a "cleansing of the house." "We were skeptical," says Lynn, "but loved their warm intentions, so we agreed."

Starting at the front of the house, they worked all through the Lemyres' new home, burning sage and gently urging whatever spirits still inhabited the house to leave and be on their way, wishing them well. When the process was completed, they all went back to the front door and saw that the family pictures that were on a table in the front hall had all been turned face down.

"Not knocked down, but almost carefully laid face down," Lynn described. Nobody else was at home, and all participants had stayed together throughout the cleansing ceremony.

"We've never had any incidences since, and I'm actually disappointed," laments Lynn. "It might have been interesting to live with them for a while!"

Well, spirits are not totally out of their lives. The Lemyres also own a gallery in town that showcases their art as well as that of other local artists who work in a variety of media. Home Fine Art, located in a beautifully restored historic building at 2 Church Street, is part of the highly spirit-active Mill Race Village section of town. Both classic and eclectic, Home Fine Art provides artistic culture to the community with exhibits and openings, concerts of progressive music, yoga on Saturday mornings…and a few ghosts.

One October, the gallery was festively decorated for Halloween, with garlands, pictures and a pumpkin head doll that stood in the corner of one of the gallery rooms. Andrew MacIver was sitting in the gallery one quiet autumn afternoon, working on the computer in the office, located in the back of the gallery. He was engrossed in his work, alone all afternoon, as no customers had come into the shop. Lemyre describes MacIver as "never a believer in ghosts and he really is a pretty pragmatic 'show me' kind of person." So when Andrew turned around and saw the pumpkin head doll standing directly behind his chair, a good ten feet or more from where it had been standing in the other room, well, let's just say his pragmatism was certainly put to the test that day.

Bill and Nina Gee are more sensitive to spirit activity than Andrew, having been victims of poltergeists for two years in their own home in nearby Burlington. Nina is a photographer and an artist whose work is often on display at Home Fine Art. Bill, who manages music events held there, has also been trained in spiritual response therapy (SRT) and has performed SRT at the gallery. He describes this process as "primarily used to clear karmic programs from a person's soul so that they can then live to

Ghosts feel at home at this haunted gallery.

their highest potential. It can also be used to clear out unwanted spirits and communicate with the other side."

Nina says,

> *At the gallery, I only felt very uncomfortable, which had always been my first impression when stuff was going on at home. On occasion I would see, fleetingly, a man dressed in a black suit with a black hat…not a top hat; maybe something more like a fedora. Sometimes he carried papers. He appeared mostly near or in the bathroom and by the solid wall where you could turn right or left into the two gallery spaces. I never got a feeling of anything bad, as I did often at home. But it is still uncomfortable for me to sit in the gallery, so I know that there is some activity…maybe more upstairs than down? Didn't that wall by the two gallery spaces lead to the upstairs at one point?*

Years ago, there was a stairway that led from what is now the art gallery to what is now an upstairs apartment. Today, there is no way to get to the upstairs from inside the gallery. The staircase was in the hallway between the two gallery rooms, which may explain why there is so much activity in that particular spot. The "group room," the largest exhibit room and where concerts are held, was the main dining room of the house.

Bill adds,

> *I only did a little SRT at the gallery so there is still plenty of activity there. In the fall of 2007, after one of the Home Stage concerts for "Pride Night" there was a considerable increase in activity both during and after the concert. So much so that at least two audience members reported some "cold spots" in the group room and by the front door of the gallery. As I was cleaning up, I sensed the presence of a woman who was quite displeased with the music!*
>
> *It's been my experience that those rooms where people experienced strong emotions (either good or bad) are usually the places where ghosts like to hang out. Therefore, places where they met and gathered are of particular interest. My theory is that the spirits are trying to work out the experiences in the afterlife by replaying these scenes over and over again until they can come to peace with it. Rarely are the spirits even aware of us, which is why they sometimes appear to walk through walls because when they were alive, a wall didn't exist there.*

Nina and Bill believe that the spirits of the gallery are harmless. They like to make noise on the second floor in the daytime and they tend to

112

gather in the hallway and dining room at night. Bill believes an elderly lady lived on the second floor and was cared for by her son or nephew, whom he believes was a bachelor and is the man Nina saw in the hat. He also senses that the lady upstairs was a shut-in either by choice or due to a chronic medical condition. There was a servant woman of Irish or Eastern European descent who ran the kitchen and rarely wandered anywhere else in the house, because "her energy in the office is pretty weak except that she liked things very orderly and tends to get out of sorts when the room is a mess. One thing I was clear on was that the man was never permitted in the kitchen."

Could she have put Andrew's pumpkin head doll where she felt it belonged when she was tidying up?

Home Fine Art's tagline is "Home Is Where the Art Is." Looks like it is also where the ghosts are.

Mediumship

Connecting with Those in Another Dimension

"And what the dead had no speech for, when living, They can tell you, being dead: the communication of the dead is tongued with fire beyond the language of the living."
—*T.S. Eliot*

J amie Faith Eachus has been intuitive since she was three years old. It began with precognitive dreams and high levels of sensitivity. Then, sometime before her tenth birthday, Jamie "shut down." She became too sensitive and, being caught in the throes of an abusive childhood, what was a "gift" became too much for her to bear. She withdrew from her sensitivity, as a means of self-protection from what was going on around her. Then, in her mid-twenties, she began to receive, or maybe, accept the spiritual energy again. After joining South Jersey Ghost Research (SJGR) in 2003, she found a safe environment to utilize her skills, resolve issues in her life and share her gift with others.

Today, Jamie is SJGR's assistant director, helping others connect with lost loved ones. She also teaches those willing to cultivate their own skills and natural abilities to communicate with the spirits of loved ones and others who have "crossed over." Does everyone have this ability, at least to some extent? Jamie believes they do.

"It depends upon true openness, your background and upbringing, as well as your past lives. If you were persecuted in your past lives, this could cause your ability and sensitivity to shut down," she says. Also, at different points in your current life, you could be more sensitive than others, depending on your emotions or situation at the time. Children are often more sensitive to spirits since they have not yet been "culturized' to not believe; they trust their feelings. Some people can have many encounters in their lives; some may only have one. Many never will, or they will not recognize it if it does occur.

Some will be intuitive, or psychic, but not possess medium capabilities. Jamie explains, "I really didn't start seeing ghosts until I was older. Every medium starts out being psychic first, but not all psychics are mediums. I was definitely intuitive long before I honed the mediumship gift that was latent within me."

Even though today they are sometimes employed by law enforcement departments to crack difficult criminal cases, mediums still sometimes get a bum rap, accused of faking responses and setting up "sitters" (a term sometimes used to describe the clients of a medium or participants in a séance).

"Alleged mediums may be able to gain information about their clients… via normal means and then use this information to help produce accurate readings," write Ciaran O'Keefe and Richard Wiseman in a 2005 article published in the *British Journal of Psychology*. They go on to say that the medium has at his or her disposal such devices as "secretly eaves-dropping on their conversations or conducting surreptitious searches of telephone directories and the Internet."

Sure, there are fake mediums as there are phonies in any field. But Jamie has done random readings during presentations at most of the Haunted Holly Ghost Tours held in Mount Holly, in front of over 120 people she had never met before. Here, she made contact with deceased loved ones of several of those in the audience. As Jamie made spirit connections, these people identified the spirits, some being brought to tears by the messages she relayed to them.

If you have the desire to communicate with loved ones who have departed this life, you can be trained to enhance whatever natural gifts you may already possess. Some mediums, like Jamie, offer classes and workshops for learning to use your natural abilities in this way. If you want to discover your innate intuitive powers and reach out to those on other spiritual planes, Jamie suggests that you be open. Be truly ready to connect in any way that person or spirit may want to connect with you. Be aware that if you are truly entrenched in grief, you may not be able to connect at that time. Ask your loved one for signs. Release all expectations; don't put conditions on the spirit, such as "if you are here, speak to me," or "show me you are here by moving that chair." The spirit will connect with you in its own way, when ready. Your loved one's spirit will most likely come to you when you are calm.

Signs of contact may come in various forms, such as:

VISUAL: Often these are in the form of dreams. In your sleep, you are most relaxed, and therefore, more receptive to messages. But you can also receive visual signs when you are awake, which may not be what you expect. Be aware of these subtle messages. Maybe you and your grandfather shared

Random readings by a medium are part of the Haunted Holly Ghost Tour. *Photo by Larry Tigar.*

a love of birds and he particularly liked Baltimore orioles. If three days after his death an oriole flew by you, especially if you do not commonly see orioles, that could very well be a sign. Be open to and aware of these vestiges.

AUDIBLE: You may overhear a conversation that is so relevant to your lost loved one, it cannot be overlooked. Jamie cites an example in her life.

When my dad died, I so wanted to hear from him and know he was there. He died of mantel cell lymphoma (a rare form of lymphoma). I was in a restaurant and overheard a conversation behind me. The person was talking about mantel cell lymphoma. Then I heard them say "forty-nine." That was my dad's age when he died. Then they said the name "Dave." That was my dad's name. Hearing just one of those snippets of conversation would not necessarily be any cause to sense anything, but all three of them together in that short conversation I just happened to overhear made me realize that this was a sign from my dad. He was using these people and this conversation to let me know he was still with me.

MUSIC: A favorite song or musician could be your loved one saying hello.

SMELLS: These are very common. Food smells, cigar smells, perfume, any smell that you relate to that person could be a sign. Smells are a common sign of residual spirit energy as well.

TEMPERATURE: Like signs of spiritual energy in haunted buildings, temperature change may indicate your loved one is near. This is most common when a feeling of warmth surrounds you, like a hug. If you are missing your lost pet, you may feel a brush by your legs, indicating your pet's spirit is near.

TASTE: Sometimes when working with a client, a medium may have a "clair sentrist" experience, meaning the medium will get a strong taste of a flavor that relates to your loved one. Jamie has gotten a taste in her mouth of tobacco if the person was a smoker, or chocolate or cherries if they were favorite flavors. This, however, is not that common.

Jamie also cautions those who are trying to contact spirits on their own. Most importantly, be sure you are in a place where you feel safe and surrounded by positive energy. She especially cautions you not to do this in a place such as a cemetery. Why not? "There is so much energy, grief and anger in places like that. You do not know what the residual energy can summon forth."

Likewise, do not use a Ouija Board. Yes, those intriguing toys of the sixties; you swore your brother was pushing the planchette and he swore you were. Actually not toys, Ouija Boards can really be powerful tools if used in the correct (or maybe incorrect) fashion. Dave Juliano, SJGR director, agrees. "It's like opening your door at three in the morning. You don't know who will be there," he says. With a Ouija Board, not only the spirit of the person you are calling may come through. You may invite evil spirits into your home that may not want to leave.

Jamie often suggests working with angels. Angels are celestial beings; they have never walked the earth. They come directly from "the source," depending on your beliefs, and they are there for you to connect to your own inner guidance. You can be trained to connect with angels. You do not pray to angels; they are messengers. Jamie likes to refer to them as "postal workers." An Angel Board can be used to connect to angels; this is not the same as a Ouija Board.

Jamie and some other mediums work with angels to help people "get in touch with the knowledge and gifts that you already know on a soul level, but may have forgotten over lifetimes of incarnations." She communicates with angels in these sessions to empower clients to move through the challenges and stumbling blocks that they are facing so that they may learn those lessons they were "contracted to learn prior to incarnating this lifetime." She channels messages from the angels to bring forth their guidance. Clients are encouraged to ask specific questions from the angels or leave it up to the angels to communicate whatever needs to come through, based on what "they" feel you need to know at this point in your life.

Jamie also strongly advocates the importance of paying attention to your "psychic hygiene"; in other words, keep a positive state of mind, always protect yourself and remain in a positive space. Some people use crystals to cleanse themselves of negative energy. Just as if you don't keep yourself physically clean you can become ill, if you don't mind your psychic hygiene, your emotional and spiritual psyche can also become ill. Good psychic hygiene will also ensure more effective readings without sacrificing your own energetic well-being.

One reason mediums may encounter so many messages from the dead is because deceased persons flock to mediums. They feel the medium is sensitive and the spirit wants to be heard.

What does a spirit go through? One thing mediums and others believe, as explained by Jamie and Dave Juliano, is that upon death, a soul goes through "life review." Here, they revisit all their interactions and feel the impact they had.

In an experiment cited by Tom Butler of the Academy of Spirituality and Paranormal Studies, which he feels illustrates what near-death researchers are finding, departed souls were asked what they experience when they die. Using electronic voice phenomenon (EVPs), the reply was, "Review our lives." In other experiments he cites, the spirits were asked, "What were some of the misconceptions about death and/or life on the other side?" Responses included "regrets" and "you're alive."

The influence and power a medium has is based on his or her ability to gather energy, and this leads to the quality of the experience and what is experienced by whom. The ability to manage this subtle energy can be developed by some people, but others naturally excel at it, or as Jamie describes it, they have "the gift." Some, such as Tom Butler, believe that a medium is thought to gather ectoplasmic energy from her sitters and form a voice box for direct-voice phenomena.

A 2001 study cited by O'Keefe and Wiseman found that almost 30 percent of Americans believe in genuine mediumship capabilities, while approximately 10 percent of our friends "across the pond" visit mediums to receive messages from the deceased as well as for guidance for their own lives. Popularity may have even grown since that survey was taken, if one is to consider new TV shows and the general popularity of card readers and mediums for both serious and recreational consultations today. In Mount Holly, regular card reading events in restaurants and at special events attract many hoping to seek guidance in their lives and ask about loved ones both living and dead. Jamie reminds us that if we seek the advice of mediums or try it ourselves, "it all comes down to intention." Be open and be safe. Don't put demands on the spirit. Don't expect your lost loved one to manifest like Patrick Swayze in *Ghost*; that's Hollywood. Let the spirits give you a sign on their own terms. Stay open and ready for it to happen.

Who Ya Gonna Call?

The Science of Professional Paranormal Research

"I don't believe in demanding that a ghost appear by taunting them. I feel that they were once human too, and deserve our respect as if they were still here. And believe it or not, when I ask if I can take their picture, I get more results."
—Garden State Ghost Hunters Society website

Mount Holly has become a destination for many ghost research groups. South Jersey Ghost Research (SJGR) has labeled our historic town a "hotbed of ghostly activity." This may be due to the rich history of Mount Holly or maybe because the spirits have just enjoyed themselves so much here they hate to leave, even though their lease on life has expired. For whatever reason, the probability that spirits do tend to linger here gains credence by the amount of paranormal research conducted in both the public buildings and the private homes of Mount Holly. Both South Jersey Ghost Research and Garden State Ghost Hunters Society support the town's regular Friday the thirteenth Haunted Holly Ghost Tour because of the strong evidence of paranormal activity they have found here.

While many are skeptical about the existence of ghosts and some refuse to believe at all, there is a science to detecting paranormal activity that is widely used. This discipline includes equipment, methods and protocols employed by those who have been trained and certified in researching paranormal phenomena. While some of the ghost stories of Mount Holly may be legend- or story-based, most are told by those who have actually experienced hauntings firsthand. Many of these haunted stories are backed up by the frequent investigations professional ghost researchers have conducted in this highly spirit-active town.

The argument of whether the study of the paranormal can be considered scientific has quite a bit of history itself, and can be traced back to the days of René Descartes and Sir Isaac Newton, when these two philosopher/ scientists and their followers argued the principles of natural law and the science of motion and matter. The argument of what is scientific and what is not accompanies scientific evolution itself, through the Darwin principles and into the birth of modern spiritualism and the science of psychology, both around the mid-1800s. Modern spiritualism, a science that supports the theory of communication with spirits of the dead, originated when three sisters bought a cabin in Hydesville, New York, in 1848 and were haunted by a rapping noise believed to be made by the ghost of a salesman who lived there before them. Modern spiritualism, which was not based on any established religion, dealt directly with the Cartesian principles of mind and the supernatural, and had some scientists in the late nineteenth century actually studying the paranormal. Some, James Beichler writes in "Trend or Trendy?" feel that modern spiritualism was an integral part of science, with its existence paralleling the more obvious scientific successes of the period.

While all this was going on in the United States, ghost hunting started in English castles in the 1860s, as Great Britain also went through a period of spiritualism and began to employ séances and planchettes (forerunners of the Ouija Board) to communicate with spirits. After a couple of decades of amateur study, the Society for Psychical Study was formed by some Cambridge scholars in an attempt to rationally study the haunting phenomena, Coulombe writes in *Haunted Castles of the World*.

In the 1930s, parapsychology, the study of the paranormal, emerged as a laboratory science under the direction of J.B. Rhine and was influenced by quantum theory, psychology and discoveries and theories on electromagnetic waves. Beichler claims that parapsychology was finally legitimized as a science in 1969 when the Parapsychology Association was admitted to the American Association for the Advancement of Science. While parapsychology may bring a level of empirical validation to some scientists since the early to mid-twentieth century, it was probably the birth of modern spiritualism that led to the development of professional paranormal research that is continually being perfected to this day.

Most respectable paranormal research organizations today exist to reveal the truth about ghosts as well as to help those who feel their home or business is being haunted and are not sure how to coexist with lingering spirits. They do not exist to convince you to believe in ghosts, and many are skeptics themselves.

Says SJGR Director Dave Juliano, "My main goal is to assist anyone that is in fear of spirit activity in their home." Assistant Director Jamie Faith

Eachus, also a medium, goes on to say, "I strive to ease the minds of clients and assist with discerning what exactly is going on in their homes so that they may better understand the events and coexist with the activity that is taking place."

South Jersey Ghost Research has been hunting ghosts in the Garden State since 1955. Emerging as a group called Ghost Hunters of America (GHA), it was formed by Hildred Robinette of Beverly, New Jersey, another town in Burlington County, about a ten-mile drive from Mount Holly. Dave Juliano had been ghost hunting since his late teens. He grew up in a haunted house and was terrified as a child of the spirit activity there. So as he got older he tried to understand what was going on and formed a group he called GHOST to work with others on investigating and understanding paranormal activity. He joined up with Robinette in the late 1990s. The groups merged and formed South Jersey Ghost Research. Juliano has been the organization's director since its inception. Many of the current ghost hunting groups in South Jersey are actually spinoffs of SJGR, which is today the Delaware Valley's oldest active paranormal research group.

Ghost researchers come from all walks of life. From law enforcement to nursing, IT to PR, vet techs, engineers and others, most hold normal day jobs of many varieties. What they have in common is that they have harbored a keen interest in the paranormal most of their lives. Some have been haunted themselves, as Juliano was in his childhood. Some were skeptics turned believers due to an incident that happened to them or a family member that seemed to exorcize their skepticism and pique their interest in finding out more, and doing it in a scientific matter. These trained investigators and consultants believe in the existence of the paranormal, and when investigating a potential "haunt" are out to scientifically prove whether spirits or residual energy are really on location.

Juliano writes in *Ghost Research 101*, "Most of this is not rocket science, but there is a definite methodology to it." By this he means he can teach anyone to read an EMF meter and anyone can tell if the temperature drops suddenly, but it is the combination of using the tools and methodologies together, ruling out external factors that result in false positives and all the other protocols used in ghost research that are important to determining the true presence of spirit energy.

SJGR has a rigorous training program for those who wish to be certified investigators. Similar programs are employed by most organizations who take their work, proving the presence of paranormal activity, seriously. According to its website, SJGR's program requires cemetery training investigations, indoor investigation training, equipment training, introduction to psychic protection/development training, EVP training, additional classroom sessions, a score of at least an eighty on a written test, passing a practical exam and a three-month probationary period.

Although South Jersey Ghost Researchers claim "all you really need is a camera and an open mind," they, and most other serious paranormal research groups, use an array of state-of-the-art equipment to verify their findings. Equipment is field tested prior to embarking on an investigation. Some of the equipment most commonly used for specter detection by these ghost hunters includes cameras, video cameras, audio recorders, electromagnetic field detectors, thermometers, motion detectors, two-way radios and flashlights with red lenses.

Juliano distinguishes between ghost hunting and ghost investigation. Ghost hunting is when you go to a place where there have been no sightings, but you are trying to catch some evidence. Ghost investigation, on the other hand, is going to a known place and recording evidence. It is often done with intent to assist the home or business owner with confirming suspected spirit activity and subsequently advising him how to deal with it.

How do you know if something strange could be a spirit trying to make contact with you? Ghosts manifest themselves in various ways. If you've experienced any of the following, you may have been touched by a ghost:

APPARITION: the supernatural appearance of a dead person or animal. Apparitions are rare.

COMMUNICATION FROM THE DEAD VIA TELEPHONE: alleged contact from the "other side" has been reported throughout history. Spirits will use any means available to them if they want to contact you. With the advent of electromagnetic technology, spirit communication has been reported via telegraph, telephone, radio and computers.

DOORS, CABINETS AND CUPBOARDS OPENING AND CLOSING: most often, these phenomena are not seen directly, but the distinct sound is heard.

EVP (ELECTRONIC VOICE PHENOMENA): EVPs, picked up on recorders, are one of the best pieces of evidence to an investigator. It is hard to dispute this evidence, as they are often in a decibel range that a human voice cannot make. They help an investigator determine the nature and identity of a spirit.

FEELINGS OF BEING WATCHED: can be attributed to the paranormal depending on where and when it happens.

MISTS: fog or smoke-like substance hanging in the air. Mists are often not visible at the time of snapping the photo, and they are much less common than orbs.

MOVEMENT OF STATIONARY OBJECTS: often reported. Spirits could be doing this to get your attention. Is there any significance to the objects that are moved? Moving of large objects could indicate more than one spirit.

ODORS: can indicate the presence of a spirit. Cigar smoke, perfume and food smells are common. Unpleasant odors such as feces, ammonia or decay could indicate the presence of a negative spirit.

ORBS: balls of energy that are found in the semi-infrared spectrum of light. The movement of the orb may be the energy being transferred from a source (power lines, heat energy, batteries, even people). You will often not see them until after a photo is processed, because the camera captures the image as pure energy.

PHYSICAL CONTACT: tapping, pulling, hair pulling are common. If it is forceful, it could be a negative spirit.

PLUMBING PROBLEMS: leaks, flooding sinks and toilets. Spirits seem to like to play with plumbing; flushing toilets and turning on faucets are often reported.

PROBLEMS WITH ELECTRICAL SYSTEMS OR APPLIANCES: spirit activity can affect anything electrical.

SOUNDS: footsteps, tapping, banging, etc. Be careful to rule out natural causes. If these are from paranormal sources, it is not uncommon for them to occur in patterns of three. You could also hear voices, although sometimes spirit voices are not within a decibel range audible by the human ear. These are often caught on tape.

STRANGE ANIMAL BEHAVIOR: a dog, cat or other pet behaves strangely. Dogs may bark at something unseen or refuse to enter a room. Cats may seem to be "watching" something cross a room or playing with unseen objects. Animals have sharper senses than humans, and are often more aware of spirit activity that the rest of the family doesn't see.

TEMPERATURE FLUCTUATIONS: uncommon hot or cold spots can indicate a spirit is present. Moving cold spots can mean a spirit is moving about the building.

UNEXPLAINED SHADOWS: the sighting of fleeting shapes and shadows, usually seen out of the corner of the eye. Oftentimes the shadows have vaguely human forms, while other times they are less distinguishable.

VORTEX: a very uncommon photo that looks like a funnel or tornado. It is believed to be an orb or multiple orbs moving at a high rate of speed.

If you have investigated a location that you really feel is haunted, but have obtained no evidence, Juliano advises in *Ghost Research 101*, "Do not assume that there are no spirits there. You can only assume that they did not interact with you and that you did not obtain any evidence of spirit activity."

But the last thing a good paranormal researcher wants to do is compromise his reputation by validating that a sight is haunted, when in actuality the evidence he has gotten is suspect, at best. After an investigation, a respectable paranormal research organization will carefully review the evidence, as well as the conditions under which the investigation was conducted. If he is not absolutely positive of what he heard, saw, felt or recorded, the research is discarded. Juliano's rule of thumb is, "When in doubt, throw it out."

This belief is generally held by most respectable paranormal researchers and scientists. Tom Butler, in an article from the 2007 Annual Conference of the Academy of Spirituality and Paranormal Research Studies, wrote, "We would rather see a researcher fail to replicate our experiments than to present misleading results."

For those interested in giving ghost hunting a try before enlisting in a professional paranormal research group, Garden State Ghost Research Society has conducted several investigations open to the public at the Burlington County Prison Museum in Mount Holly. Here they set up exhibits and lecture on ghost investigating practices prior to taking interested individuals on an actual investigation of the site, using some of their equipment such as EMF detectors, thermal scanners and infrared lights. During these investigations, amateurs are accompanied by the professionals and witness firsthand what an investigation is all about. Their website claims that some of the attendees have even been "touched and or had their shirts tugged at," all the while learning how to objectively and scientifically discern if paranormal activity is present.

Why are they doing it in Mount Holly? Because that's where the ghosts are!

Why Exit?

"It's not that I'm afraid to die. I just don't want to be there when it happens."
—Woody Allen

If you live in New Jersey, you're probably tired of hearing "what exit?" from those who have spent little time here and think we are nothing more than the New Jersey Turnpike or the Garden State Parkway.

But as you can see, Mount Holly ghosts know better, asking instead, "Why exit?" Why exit this state of seashores, quaint towns, interestingly diverse cities and colorful farmland? Even the Garden State Parkway reportedly has a phantom, lingering on the northbound lane around exit 82.

It seems that no matter where you go in Mount Holly, there they are. Men, women, dogs, cats, unable to exit, clinging to a town they just can't leave behind. Whether or not you believe the stories of the residents and workers in Mount Holly, experiences backed up by the evidence of professionally trained ghost researchers and the history that has been here for centuries, something is happening here, and something has been happening here for a long time.

Dave Juliano told me, "There is nothing you can do to convince a skeptic." True; but there sure are enough people here who have experienced Mount Holly's afterlife firsthand and don't need to be convinced of anything.

The ghosts of Mount Holly don't plan on leaving anytime soon. They've enjoyed the afterlife here for centuries. Come meet them; hear their stories every Friday the thirteenth. They're waiting for you, Turnpike exit 5.

Bibliography

About.com: Paranormal Phenomena website. "16 Signs That Your House is Haunted." http://paranormal.about.com/od/ghosthuntinggeninfo/a/aa060704.htm.

Association of the Bar of the City of New York Library. "Crimes of Passion." http://www.abcny.org/Library/FeaturedExhibitions4.htm.

Beck, Henry Charlton. "*The Jersey Midlands*." New Brunswick, NJ: Rutgers University Press, 1962.

Beichler, James E., PhD. "Trend or Trendy? The Development and Acceptance of the Paranormal by the Scientific Community." *The Journal of Spirituality and Paranormal Studies* 30, no. 1 (January 2007): 41–58.

Berbauer, Thomas A. "Arney's Mount Historian Enjoys Lifestyle of the Past." *Courier Post*, November 2, 2007.

Bicentennial Committee of the Colonel Thomas A. Reynolds Chapter of the National Society of the Daughters of the American Revolution. *Historic Mount Holly: The Holly Tour.* Sleeper Publications, 1975; reprinted by Burlington County College, 2002.

Bressman, Paola. *Applied Cognitive Psychology* 16, no. 1 (January 2002): 17–34.

Britt, Robert Roy. "Higher Education Fuels Stronger Belief in Ghosts." LiveScience website, http://www.livescience.com/strangenews/060121_paranormal_poll.html.

Burlington County History and Tourism, http://www.co.burlington.nj.us/tourism/history/looptour/african.htm.

Burlington County Prison Museum Assocation. Online brochure, http://www.co.burlington.nj.us/departments/resource_conservation/parks/sites/museum/brochure/index.htm.

———. Reprint of the Authentic Confession of Joel Clough. Originally published by Sheriff of Burlington County, 1833.

———. Reprint of "A History of Wesley Warner's Crime, The Murder of Lizzie Peak, 1894, Mount Holly."

Butler, Tom. "What We Know About Life After Death." Academy of Spirituality and Paranormal Studies, Inc., Annual Conference, 2007.

Charles Dickens, Gad Hill's Place website, http://www.perryweb.com/Dickens/.

Coulombe, Charles A. *Haunted Castles of the World*. Guilford, CT: The Lyons Press, 2004.

Court TV Crime Library, http://www.crimelibrary.com/criminal_mind/psychology/insanity/2/html).

Derry, Ellis L. *Old and Historic Churches of New Jersey, Vol. 1*. Medford, NJ: Plexus Publishing, Inc., 2003.

Garden State Ghost Hunters Society website, http://www.gsghs.com.

Ghost Hunting 101 website, http://www.ghosthunting101.com/.

Guiley, Rosemary Ellen. *The Encyclopedia of Ghosts and Spirits*. New York: Facts on File, Inc., 1992.

Harris Interactive website, http://www.harrisinteractive.com.

Hughes, Mathew, Robert Behanna and Margaret L. Signorella. "Perceived Accuracy of Fortune Telling and Belief in the Paranormal." *Journal of Social Psychology* 141, no. 1 (February 2001): 159–60.

Interment.net website, http://www.interment.net/Default.htm

Juliano, Dave. *Ghost Research 101: Investigating Haunted Homes*. Shadows Publishing, 2005.

Levins, Hoag. Historic Camden County News. http://historiccamdencounty.com/ccnews11.shtml.

Main Street Mount Holly. Pamphlet for the Hidden Gardens of Mount Holly. June 9, 2006.

Milbourne, Christopher, and Maurine Milbourne. *The Illustrated History of Magic*. New York: Carroll & Graf, 2005.

Moore, David W. "Three in Four Americans Believe in the Paranormal." Gallup News Service. Princeton, NJ: The Gallup Organization.

Moran, Mark, and Mark Sceurman. *Weird NJ, Volume 2*. New York: Sterling Publishing Company, 2006.

Museum of Hoaxes website, http://www.museumofhoaxes.com.

New York Times, February 28, 1929.

O'Keefe, Ciaran, and Richard Wiseman. "Testing Alleged Mediumship: Methods and Results." *British Journal of Psychology*. 2005.

Perinchief, Elizabeth M. *History of Cemeteries in Burlington County, N.J., 1687–1975*. Mount Holly, NJ, 1978.

Rizzo, Dennis C. *Mount Holly, New Jersey: A Hometown Reinvented*. Charleston, SC: The History Press, 2007.

Sacred Texts.com website, http://www.sacred-texts.com.

The SF Site: A conversation with Leslie What, http://www.sfsite.com/07b/lw132.htm.

Shinn, Henry C. *The History of Mount Holly*. Mount Holly, NJ: Mount Holly Herald, 1957.

South Jersey Ghost Research. "Collective Investigation Report—Case #01-062." Relief Fire Engine Co, Mount Holly, NJ. September 8, 2001.

South Jersey Ghost Research website, http://www.southjerseyghostresearch.org

South Jersey Paranormal Research website, http://www.sjpr.org.

Winzinger, Heidi J., and Mary L. Smith. *Images of America: Mount Holly*. Charleston, SC: Arcadia, 2001.